**3:16 Power!**

**By**

**Mo Mydlo**

ISBN: 9798666489420

## Dedication

This devotional is dedicated to every believer in Jesus Christ who has been martyred for their faith. Every one of us who are free in Christ are eternally indebted to you. May those of us who are free in Christ keep the Great Commission our highest priority until we meet Jesus face to face someday in Heaven.

## Acknowledgments

I want to thank Holy Spirit for His love, His guidance, and His creativity in writing this devotional.

I want to thank My husband Tommy for his patience and his encouragement of me to finish this book. I was distracted many times by the needs of the ministry and my unending desire to loiter in the garden.

I want to thank my beautiful friend Jean Hammond for proofreading yet another Mo Mydlo devotional. You are a spectacular friend Jean Jean.

I want to thank my extremely, talented friend Lesa Schwartz for creating the cover art for this book. Our ministry has been blessed beyond measure because of your many gifts and talents in serving The Lord.

# Introduction

We have all seen the John 3:16 signs held up by fans at football games and sporting events.  But, do we take the time to ponder in our heart of hearts the power that those three numbers represent? Do we find ourselves moved to inquire just why people will hold up a handmade sign for hours, just hoping to get a second of exposure on a local or national television network?

What moves people to memorize John 3:16, make it their life verse or tattoo it on their skin? I would venture to guess it is because it represents some sort of change in their own lives. John 3:16 is a powerful verse. It changes all our lives. It changes lives here on Earth and in Heaven.  Most Christians are aware of the significance of the verse John 3:16, *For God so loved the world that he gave his one and only Son, that whoever believes in him shall not perish but have eternal life.* We are saved by grace, through faith because of the love that God has for us.  John 3:16 means everything to a believer who has made Jesus Lord.

Through the study of God's Word, the Holy Spirit has shown me just how amazing John 3:16 is. He also made clear to me, and I pray that He will reveal to you as well, that the third chapter and sixteenth verse of each book of the Bible is powerful and has eternal significance as well.  As I studied each book of the Bible personally, the third chapter and sixteenth verse seemed to pack a powerful faith punch that left my jaw dropping and my heart stirred to dig deeper in study and prayer.

I had no doubt that God wanted me to name this devotional *3:16 Power*. There is power in the Word of God to break the strongholds of the enemy. There is power in the Word of God to heal. There is power in the Word of God to save, redeem, restore, and to set the captives free. There is power in the Name of Jesus and in The Word of God. It is my prayer that you discover the power made available to you as a child of God.

If you are a disciple of Jesus Christ, you literally carry Christ with you. Holy Spirit now resides inside of you because you have believed the truth of God's love for you displayed in John 3:16. As you read this devotional you will be joining me in studying the other amazingly, powerful truths hidden in the third chapter and sixteenth verse of each book of the Bible. I pray that your quiet time with God becomes ignited with Holy Spirit,3:16 power.

# It's Born in Us

## Genesis 3:16

*To the woman he said, "I will greatly increase your pains in childbearing; With pain you will give birth to children. Your desire will be for your husband, And he will rule over you."*

Ever wondered why little baby girls are so inclined to grab baby dolls and try to cuddle them, carry them around close to their chests and sometimes even mimic mommy breastfeeding or bottle feeding? It's a precious sight to see and an amazing testimony of God's innate desire that He placed in little girls to nurture others.

Two of my sons are grown now. They go to college full time and work full time. They both have chosen amazing women to pursue as future wives. These two ladies love Jesus, they are hard workers, they love their families and they obviously love my sons. It is comforting to my heart to watch these women find the amazing qualities in my boys that of course as a mama, I can see easily. Mommies do not have a problem thinking their children are tremendous.

Today my son Travis had a day off work and a few hours before his classes and his girlfriend showed up ready to work. She said, "We are going to clean his room today and get organized." My cleaning genes smiled from the inside out. I thought, "Praise God from whom all blessings flow." They are in there right now, organizing closets, vacuuming corners and dusting. These sounds are like music to my ears. Every once in a while, I hear her say, "Oh, my goodness." I can only venture to guess what she found under the bed or in the corner of a closet.

As I read Genesis 3:16 today I realized, how amazing this scripture is. At first, we may think, *Oh yes, thanks a lot Eve, now we get the pains of childbirth.* But, I looked at it differently today. I thought *Praise God, we get to be the nurturers, the bearers of children in our womb, the ones that help our amazing men realize that socks should only be worn one time and not stuffed in our sneakers to re-wear. We get to daydream about the men we can't wait to walk down the aisle with and the future children that will have both of our features. We get to, not have to.*

How amazing is our God? Though He offered discipline in this scripture, once again His discipline is covered in loving grace and mercy. We were actually blessed as women by God in this powerful passage. He allowed us to be wives and mothers and lovers of others.

Now if you will excuse me, I can't wait to hear what she found in his room.

**Prayer focus: Thank God today for the precious gift of being a wife and a mother. Thank God for your mother.**

**Now that's 3:16 Power!**

## He Saw

### Exodus 3:16

*Go, assemble the elders of Israel and say to them, 'The LORD, the God of your fathers—the God of Abraham, Isaac and Jacob—appeared to me and said: I have watched over you and have seen what has been done to you in Egypt.*

When God appeared to Moses in the burning bush I can only imagine the fear, amazement and pure jaw- dropping feeling he experienced as God showed up in such a miraculous way to let His people know; the great I Am is on the scene. I love God's creativity. He could have sent an angel. He could have transformed from a dove into a human. He is God, He could have done anything. This time He chose to light a bush on fire and speak through it. He's too cool.

What does He come to tell Moses? He is so good and loving and faithful. He shows up to let him and the Israelites know in so many words, *Don't worry, I got this.* He wanted His people to know, that what happened to them, all those years in slavery, didn't escape His view. He wanted them to know it's time for their freedom and it's time for them to walk into their promised land.

Do you ever feel like God hasn't seen your situation? Have you ever felt like He has left you to handle this life on your own? Do you ever feel abandoned and alone? Ever feel like your prayers are bouncing off the ceiling?

My friend, this scripture is proof that God is right with us in our midst. He is not a separated, unfeeling God who doesn't care about our struggles. He is a God that is keeping record so He can show up at just the right time. *Psalm 56:8 (NLT): You keep track of all my sorrows. You have collected all my tears in your bottle. You have recorded each one in your book.*

I'm sure while the Israelites were in Egypt all of those years forced into slavery, they felt abandoned, alone and forgotten. God needed them to know the exact opposite is true. He actually said, *I watched over you.* There is just something comforting in knowing that no matter what we are going through, God has His eye on us.

Today, if you are in a situation that feels hopeless and lonely, make an effort to remember that God is with you. He is watching over you. If you have made Him Lord, He is actually in you.  He may be very quiet, but I promise you He's there. He will never leave you nor forsake you.

**Prayer focus: Today, thank God that whatever you are going through that isn't comfortable or is causing you great pain, that this too shall pass. Thank Him that He will never leave you, nor forsake you. Thank Him for catching your every tear.**

**Now that's 3:16 Power!**

# God Gets Our Best

## Leviticus 3:16

*The priest shall burn them on the alter as food, an offering made by fire, a pleasing aroma. All the fat is the Lord's.*

The book of Leviticus was so specific about how to offer sacrifices under the law, even how to cut up the offerings and what parts of the animal belonged to whom. It is so detailed and I love how we see that once there is a pleasing aroma, God gets the fattened part. Oh my goodness, God has such good taste. I have to be honest, I think that it's the fatty part of pork chops and steak that taste the best. My mom used to cringe when I would eat my sister's fatty part off of her meat. For some reason, it just tasted so good to me. It just must have been a God thing. It wasn't very healthy for me though.

I don't think that the book of Leviticus mentions this because it tasted the best to God. I think we are supposed to understand that in everything in our lives, God should get the best part, not the leftovers. We are supposed to give God our best in whatever situation we face in life. Obviously when we give of our finances, our first ten percent is supposed to go to God. That's our tithe. But how are we doing with giving God our time?

Are you giving God the best part of your day? Do you wake up and grab that cup of coffee, excited to see what His Word reveals to you today, or are you more interested in seeing what the local news channel is saying, or how many " likes" you got throughout the night on your social media post? Do you wake up and sit quietly before Him, basing your to-do list around His plans for you, or do you just get started with your plans and ask God to just bless your agenda as you pull out of the driveway?

The truth is, God should be getting our best, but most of the time, He gets our leftovers. He gets little silent, *Help me Jesus* prayers throughout the day because we allowed busyness and greed and tasks to dictate our schedule and we neglect the power of the Holy Spirit's ease that He could add to anything we do. We sacrifice God's grace to get out ahead in carpool.

How about today we give God a pleasing aroma of our time; and we cut out the best part of our day for Him? I promise you it will not be a waste your time. His holy ease will follow you through the thickness of the day. Let's give God our best today.

**Prayer focus: Ask God to show you how to carve out just a little more time for Him first thing in the morning.**

**Now that's 3:16 Power!**

# As Commanded by The Word

## Numbers 3:16

*So, Moses counted them, as he was commanded by the word of The Lord.*

In the third chapter of the book of Numbers we are smack dab in the middle of the first census ever taken. Moses was instructed by God in the Tent of Meeting to start counting the Israelites clan by clan and tribe by tribe. In chapter three we find the Levite tribe being counted. The Levites were Israelites from the tribe of Levi. Levi was the third son of Leah and Jacob. God chose the Levites to be priests and serve in the tabernacle and later the temple. The Priests were the mediators between man and God at the time.

Sometimes I bet Moses wanted to ask God *why?* God would tell him to do things, and Moses was simply obedient and did them. But, I bet he would turn around sometimes and think to himself; "this doesn't make any sense, but okay!" Have you ever been there? Do you ever wonder why God does things, when God is going to make something happen, or how it's going to happen? I do.

I am kind of one of those *over-thinkers*. I try to figure God out, and though once in a while He reveals some kind of detail to me about why I have to do something, usually He makes me come to the end of myself and just say, *"This doesn't make sense, but okay"*.

The truth is, we aren't ever going to completely figure out God. He's not human, He's God! He's not natural, He's supernatural! We do not have to figure out why, we simply must follow His commands. Moses didn't ask why He had to do the census. He just did the census. Moses understood obedience. God is glorified in our obedience.

Yesterday, Holy Spirit told me while I was worshipping, to walk over to a woman standing with our pastor's wife and pray with her. I didn't know her, but God did. I kept worshipping and in my Spirit said to God; "Okay, after service I'll pray with her." God said, "Go now!" I realized I wasn't being obedient. God was moving and doing something in her life, and I needed to be obedient immediately. So, I went to her and said; "I know you don't know me but God told me to pray for you. Is there anything specific?" She said, "I don't think so." So I just prayed for her health, for any protection she may need from the enemy, I prayed for her family and for whatever it was that God was getting ready to do in her life."

I walked away knowing I was being obedient even though I didn't really have an answer why. Later that day, our pastor's wife texted me and said, "Just so you know I agree, God sent you to pray for her." She didn't share any details and I didn't need them. I was just thankful I had listened. (Even though it took God prompting me a little).

My friend, what is God telling you to do that you have put off doing because it doesn't make sense, or you can't figure it out? Is it a book you are supposed to write or a song he has given you lyrics to or a new position you are supposed to apply for? What is it? Allow me to encourage you today to just do it. No questions asked. Even though we may not figure it out here, I have a feeling when we are in Heaven, our mouths are going to drop seeing all that God was up to. He's just so cool!

**Prayer focus: Spend time asking God to help you be obedient to His commands and calls.**

**Now that's 3:16 Power!**

# We All Have Our Lots

## Deuteronomy 3:16

*But to the Reubenites and the Gadites I gave the territory extending from Gilead down to the Arnon Gorge (the middle of the gorge being the border) and out to the Jabbok River, which is the border of the Ammonites.*

During the time of Moses, God had led His people all through the desert and when they were just about to enter the promised land, Moses took some time to address the crowd and reminisce with The Israelites about the trials and triumphs that God brought them through and then He gave them some instructions before they took their next steps.

In chapter three Moses is referring to the division of the land and how they allotted it after they would defeat an army and plunder their possessions. They were remembering all the wars that they won because of God's provision and protection of them. This is the record of the allotment for the Reubenites and Gadites.

When I read this I thought, *we all have our lots, don't we?* If we think about God's division of gifts and talents and even trials in our lives like the division of land among the Israelites we are able to realize that Ecclesiastes 9:11 is true: "I have seen something else under the sun: The race is not to the swift or the battle to the strong, nor does food come to the wise or wealth to the brilliant or favor to the learned, but time and chance happen to them all."

You see, I'm sure some of the Israelites complained that some of the tribes were given better farmland than others. Some pieces of land might have had streams and springs and some might have been drier and required more irrigation. Some lots might have had hills and mountains when others may have been flat for as far as the eye can see. But they were given land and it was a careful division of the land

and done by God's hand. Which means it was right and it could be trusted.

Often when I think about my lot in life, or like a friend of mine refers to it as "my story" that God is penning about my life, most of the time I am grateful, honored and thankful beyond my ability to voice. Then there are those days that my feelings creep in and I feel sorry for myself for having to fight the daily anxiety voices that God has allowed in my life for as long as I can remember. I begin to deal with the "why me?" voices. Do you know what I mean? Am I being too real?

When I sense myself getting into an old -fashioned pity party about the trials of life that I have faced and the hills and valleys of my lot that God has so lovingly drawn into the pages of my story, sometimes I feel God nudge me and say; "Okay, now how about some perspective?" Guess where I get my perspective. He shows me other people's lots. Because we all have them.

Our selfishness loves to zoom in on whatever junk we are dealing with and we lose focus of the truth. The truth is, we all have struggles. We all have trials. We all have God-shaped holes in our hearts that only God can fill. Some of us struggle with chronic sickness or pain or the permanent loss of a loved one until we are united in eternity. Some struggle with divorce or financial lack or hunger or habits in life. We all have our lots in life, and do you know why? Our lots are what draw us close to God. Our lots in life make us desperate for our Maker. Our lots, when handled with the proper amount of prayer and worship and the Word allow God to be glorified in us.

Wow! God is truly the giver of every good and perfect gift. He even takes our junk in life and turns it into a treasure. My friend, today will you choose to thank God for your lot in life? When God was dividing up the promised land, He knew what He was doing. Trust Him with it.

**Prayer focus:** Thank God for the good things in your life, as well as for the tough things you deal with that draw you closer to Him.

**Now that's 3:16 Power!**

# Put Your Foot In

## Joshua 3:16

*The water from upstream stopped flowing. It piled up in a heap a great distance away, at a town called Adam in the vicinity of Zarethan, while the water flowing down to the Sea of the Arabah (that is, the Dead Sea) was completely cut off. So the people crossed over opposite Jericho.*

It doesn't matter what it is that you feel God is calling you to do, there is always a first step. Maybe you feel like it's time to add to your family and have another child. After praying it through with your spouse, there are some steps you must take before the Lord places a baby in your womb, obviously.  Maybe God is calling you to sell your home, pursue a new career or even start a new ministry. Whatever it is that God is calling you to, there will be a step that you must take.

The Israelites were being led by Joshua into the Promised Land. They all followed the priests who were carrying the ark of the covenant (God's Laws). God told Joshua in Joshua 3:8, "Tell the priests who carry the ark of the covenant: 'When you reach the edge of the Jordan's waters, go and stand in the river." Okay, sounds easy enough right? Well, not so much. The Jordan River was at flood stage. These priests were asked to stand in raging floodwater.

Joshua 3:15-16 says: "Yet as soon as the priests who carried the ark reached the Jordan and their feet touched the water's edge, the water from upstream stopped flowing." Now, does this say it stopped flowing when they approached the river? No. Does this say it stopped flowing when they rebuked the river? No. It says it stopped flowing when their feet touched the water's edge.

Oh friend, you have to put your foot in. You have to take a step if you want the blessings that God is calling you to. He's not going to lead you somewhere that He won't carry you through, but you are going to have to let Him know that you trust Him, and put your foot in.

I had no idea how to get a book published the first time I wrote a book. I just knew God told me to write it. I figured He would show me how to publish it after I wrote it, and He did. I had no idea how to write and give a message to hundreds and thousands of listeners the first time I did it, but I trusted that the God that gave me the words would help me to speak them, and He did.

You see, stepping out in faith requires literal steps. We have to put our feet in the water before God will stop the flood and allow us to walk on dry ground. He did it for the Israelites. He will do it for you. Where do you need to take a step today?

**Prayer focus: Ask God to give you the courage to take the next step that you know He is calling you to take. He will never leave you to walk it out alone. He's just waiting for you to take the first step.**

**Now that's 3:16 Power!**

# Made Perfectly for His Use

## Judges 3:16

*Now Ehud had made a double-edged sword about a foot and a half long, which he strapped to his right thigh under his clothing.*

In Judges 3 we find out that the Israelites did evil again in the eyes of the Lord, so He allowed an evil King to over them.  Here we meet the evil Eglon, King of Moab. For 18 years, the Israelites were forced to live under his rule. Then, just like we do when we can't stand our own consequences for our mess anymore, the Israelites cried out to God to help them, and He did.

The Lord sent them a man named Ehud. All we know about Ehud is that he was left -handed and he was from the tribe of Benjamin. Why does the Bible tell us that he was left- handed? Well, to be left-handed in Ehud's day was considered a handicap. I think God wanted us to know Ehud wasn't perfect, but he would be sufficient for God's use because of our Perfect God.

Do you feel insufficient for God's use? Do you believe the lie that you have to have it all together before God can use you? I tell you that's a lie because truly, no one "has it all together." We are all a mess without Jesus. We need the Lord to place His spirit in us and work through us: otherwise, we are weak and powerless.  We are incapable of any lasting good on our own. But with the Holy Spirit's guidance and supernatural power we are capable of amazing things.

Ehud was left- handed, but when he planned to take down the evil Eglon King of Moab, he strapped a sword to his right thigh. This sword was not any ordinary sword though. Judges 3:16 tells us; "Now Ehud had made a double- edged sword about a foot and a half long, which he strapped to his right thigh under his clothing."

I have no doubt that God's attention to detail in working through Ehud was in full effect. Where do we read about a double- edged sword in the bible? Two other places come right to mind with me.

Hebrews 4:12: "For the Word of God is living and active. Sharper than any double- edged sword, it penetrates even to dividing soul and spirit, joints and marrow: it judges the thoughts and attitudes of the heart." We also see in Revelation 1:16 Jesus showing up described this way; "In his right hand he held seven stars, and out of his mouth came a sharp double-edged sword."

The Word of God and Jesus are both affiliated with a double-edged sword. Do you have any doubt that Jesus was involved in the conquering of this evil king to protect the Israelites? I don't. Do you have any doubt that with the Word of God and with Jesus, you are capable of anything God calls you to do? I don't.

Ehud took down the evil king, encouraged the Israelites to follow him into victory: they struck down about ten thousand Moabites that day and The Word says; "not a man escaped." Then, from that day on Moab was subject to the Israelites and there was peace in the land for eighty years. Isn't that just like God? He does everything amazingly!

Friend, even though Ehud had what the world considered a handicap that obviously didn't matter to God. Why do you think He isn't interested in using you? Yes, I'm pretty sure that double edged sword had something to do with their victory and it will have everything to do with ours.

**Prayer focus: Spend time in prayer with God thanking Him specifically for the double- edged sword, the Word!**

**Now that's 3:16 Power!**

# Widows and Orphans

## Ruth 3:16

*When Ruth came to her mother-in-law, Naomi asked, "How did it go my daughter?*

The Book of Ruth is such an amazing testimony of sacrificial love, obedience, and God's blessings toward us when we walk out these principals. Ruth and her mother-in-law Naomi found themselves widowed at the same time. Naomi was left heartbroken; her son and her husband were taken from her and at one point she says; "Call me Mara." Mara translates as bitter. I don't think I could blame her.

Sometimes life is just not fair. Thank God that Jesus never promised us that this life would be fair or we all would walk around saying, "Call me Mara." Jesus actually promises us the opposite when He says in John 16:33: "I have told you these things, so that in me you may have peace. In this world you will have trouble. But take heart! I have overcome the world." We really aren't promised perfection. We are promised though, a Savior who has overcome all of this mess.

In Ruth 3:16 we find Naomi wondering how an encounter went in which Ruth would trust in God's provisional plan for widows by seeking her kinsman-redeemer. A kinsman-redeemer was a relative who volunteered to take responsibility for the extended family when a woman's husband died. Ruth had just returned from letting a man named Boaz know, she wished for him to be her kinsman-redeemer. This was not only a big deal for Ruth, it affected Naomi as well, since she had no other son or family members to care for her. Because of the kindness and mercy of an obvious man of God named Boaz, he did what he was called to do and he made this promise a realty in these two widow's lives.

Yes, this is a happy ending for Ruth and Naomi. God blessed them with new life again after suffering much grief. Ruth had a baby who actually ended up being King David's grandfather. His name is Obed. There's just something very healing about a new baby in the family, isn't there?

But the truth is, not all widows are given this type of restoration. Many widows struggle and face this life alone, without any relatives or close family to care for them. The church is supposed to be the place where these widows can find the support and encouragement that they need. Guess what? We are the church. We are the bride of Christ. We are supposed to care for widows and orphans. God calls this pure religion. In the book of James 1:27 we read, "Religion that God our Father accepts as pure and faultless is this: to look after orphans and widows in their distress and to keep oneself from being polluted by the world."

Are we looking after orphans and widows? Do you know a widow? Is there a neighbor, someone you know from work, or a friend of yours who is a widow? Are there children in your circle who you know who are in the foster care system, or simply do not have Godly influences in their lives? Could you be that special someone to these people?

Boaz took full responsibility for Ruth and Naomi. We aren't called to take full responsibility. We are simply called to look after these widows and orphans. Maybe you could be the one to lead them to their amazing, eternal Kinsman-Redeemer Jesus Christ.

**Prayer focus: Pray and ask God if there is a widow or orphan, or maybe a single mom or her children that you could minister to on His behalf. You will never regret a life lived for God and others.**

**Now that's 3:16 Power!**

# Tough Call from God

## 1 Samuel 3:16

*but Eli called him and said, "Samuel my son.' Samuel answered, 'Here I am'".*

This scripture starts in the middle of a sentence. I think it would be hard to study it without knowing the beginning of the sentence, as it truly does set it up. 1 Samuel 3:15 says: "Samuel lay down until morning and then opened the doors of the house of the Lord. He was afraid to tell Eli the vision."

Oh yes. We needed this detail. What was the vision? Well, it just so happens that the first time Samuel hears from God and realizes it is God and not his spiritual mentor Eli, God gives him a tough pill to swallow. He tells him that Eli is about to receive the fulfilment of a disciplinary action that he said he was going to give him for not disciplining his own disobedient boys. It almost hurts to write the seriousness of God's wrath. He says in verse 3:11: "See, I am about to do something in Israel that will make the ears of everyone who hears it tingle." Ouch! I don't think that was a good tingle.

Can you completely understand why Samuel didn't want to share this with Eli? I can! Who wants to be the one to share that news? Especially with your mentor. "Um, God's pretty ticked off." Yes, that one is a tough share. Thank God because of the sacrifice of Jesus, God isn't angry anymore. He poured his wrath out on Jesus. If we feel like we have nothing else to be thankful for some days, we should remember that! God's not mad at us anymore.

Yes, Samuel's first taste of being a prophet and spokesman for God was covered in difficulty. Do you think God did that on purpose? I do. I don't think God does anything without His ultimate purposes on the front burner. God knew Samuel's obedience needed to be tested. He tests ours with difficulties as well sometimes. Samuel passed the test. Do we?

Do we always do the hard things that God is calling us to do? Do we take the narrow roads that lead to life like the Bible talks about, or do we hop on the bandwagon in the wide and easier road because that's where all of our friends are? Even our Christian friends.

Yes, there are many things that aren't sin that we can do. But are they always the best for us? Do we always choose obedience and discipline? The answer is no. Thank God for a Savior who rescues us from our disobedience, gets us up off our skinned spiritual knees and puts us back on our feet to try again. Thank God for His grace. It's our only hope at ever getting anything right here on earth.

Yes, I believe God calls his servants like Samuel to swallow hard pills sometimes, and we are his servants as well. Don't love how yours tastes? Let me encourage you to take a big gulp of living water and get it down and press on. You can do it. We all are in this together. Stay in the race, relying heavily on grace.

**Prayer focus: Ask God to show you where you may be avoiding a narrow path that He is calling you to walk on. Plead with Him to cover you with His grace so that you can put on your faith boots and walk it out once and for all.**

**Now that's 3:16 Power!**

# All is Not Fair in Love and War

## 2 Samuel 3:16

*Her husband however, went with her, weeping behind her all the way to Bahurim. Then Abner said to him, "Go back home!" So he went back.*

You must get a little history before you can know what God is talking about in this passage. This passage is about a woman named Michal, King David's first wife. She was given to David in marriage by her father, King Saul, when David was still on Saul's good side. The second David started getting a little too much popularity with the people, our insecure King Saul (who had insane people-pleasing issues) began to despise David and wanted nothing less than to destroy him. One of the things Saul did to destroy him was, he stole his daughter back from David and gave her to another man.

David loved Michal and he wanted his wife back. Saul's commanding officer Abner was typically against David on the battle lines, but after Saul died and his son Ish-Bosheth took over Abner (who always respected David, opponent or not) decided to change sides and join David's men. David didn't know if he trusted Abner so he told him, if you are true to me, you will bring me back my wife Michal, and he did.

I don't know who to feel sorry for the most, David, Michal or her poor new husband named Paltiel son of Laish. Let's just call him Pal for short. David obviously loved Michal. He cared enough about her to fight for her back years after she was taken from his home and given to another. Then there is Michal. Oh my goodness what a feeling being totally at the mercy of whatever her father, or husband or in this case; a random officer in the military decide to do with her.

My control issues struggle with needing to know that our water bill is paid each month and that I don't have to worry about them shutting it off for non-payment. To imagine someone ripping me away from my husband, children and home and placing me in the arms of another, I'm speechless. Then there is Pal.  The Word says he was "weeping behind her all the way." Are you kidding me? A few things get to that lump in my throat like nothing else and one of them is a crying man whose heart is broken.

This story is difficult on many levels. I was praying about that and I thought, yes, life is. This story is unfair on so many levels. Yes, life is. This story hurts our core and screams: *this is not in the fairy tales I read when I was little.* Nope, life sure isn't. Life here one Earth is not fair. That old saying is not really true; *all is fair in love and war.* It's not fair.

It's not fair that,

children die of cancer

It's not fair that,

single moms raise kids alone because Dad was chasing something younger than mom down the street.

It's not fair that,

bankruptcy and divorce and foreclosure happen.

It's not fair that

loved ones die and leave us here lonely.

Life isn't fair. But God is still on His throne.

God sees our messed up, unfair, world and He isn't surprised by any of it, nor is He absent from any of our struggles and pain. Jesus said in John 16:33: "I have told you these things, so that in me you may have peace. In this world you will have trouble. But take heart! I have overcome the world." God never promised us fair, He promised us His peace. God doesn't tell us that the world will be easy. Actually He says, "In this world, you will have trouble." But He promises; He is the one that overcame it.

You see, Father God knew this world was going to be hard on us. That's why He sent us His son to die for our sins. Then when Jesus had to return to the Father, He sent us Holy Spirt to guide us after that.

It makes me think; this world takes, takes, takes with no regard for our hearts. Our God gives, gives, gives and our hearts are His top priority.

Though life isn't fair, our God is fair. He is good, He is just, He is merciful and He is loving. Our God is amazing.

**Prayer focus: Go to our God in prayer and tell Him about the things that seem unfair to you. Ask Him to show you His heart towards you. You will be surprised to find that He thinks about you and you are on His mind.**

**Now that's 3:16 Power!**

# A Mother's Love

## I Kings 3:16

### *Now two prostitutes came to the king and stood before him.*

Now, this is a crazy story. Want to hear Mo's abridged version of 1 Kings 3:16-28? Two women that lived in the same home, each had a baby. They were the only people home one evening and one of the women laid on top of her baby in her sleep and killed him. She got up, put the dead baby in the other woman's room and took the other woman's live baby and placed him at her breast. The mother of the live baby came in and said; "Give me back my baby." Well, the mother that swapped the two children said, "No, this is my baby. Yours is the dead baby." It was a "she said-she said" dilemma and these women took their argument to the king to decide.

How the king handled it is not how we see disputes handled on courtroom TV today. The King ordered for a sword to be brought to him and for the live baby to be cut into two before the women so they each could take half a baby. Let's be honest, he wasn't going to perform this deed, he was simply testing the hearts of the women.

The mother of the live baby begged for them to spare the baby and she even said; "give her the baby, just don't kill him." The mother who performed the swap was not appalled by the idea of cutting the baby into equal halves. Obviously, the King could see who the real mother was and he ordered the baby to be given back to his rightful mother. The people began to see the wisdom of this king and trusted his ability to rule.

Wow, this one will make your heart pound, won't it? Just thinking about this story makes a mother want to go grab her children and hug them tightly. Our children are our most prized possessions as mothers and we know what an honor it is to be given the title of mother. Our children are a part of us and they become much of what we make our identity to be at times.

What if someone hurts your child? This woman's child was first abducted from her, then used as a pawn in her scheme to replace her dead child, then this mother had to hear a king say the words; "Cut this child in two." What in the world do you do with these emotions? How do we process the hurt? Talk about PTSD (post-traumatic stress disorder)!

We process the pain of something traumatic happening to our child/children the same way we process any other hurt we face in life, day by day trusting God, allowing Him to be our vindicator and remembering that these children we are blessed with are actually God's and He has their best interest at heart. We remember that He will redeem whatever has been stolen or lost from them. We process the pain, fixing our eyes on Jesus and allowing God to wrap us in His love. We process the pain enjoying every second that we are given with these precious treasures, our children and pointing them to our Savior.

A mother's love is unlike any other love we have ever experienced. I believe it's the closest thing to the Father's love.

**Prayer focus: Pray for mother's everywhere. Pray especially for mothers whose children are hurting.**

**Now that's 3:16 Power!**

# Mercy Digs a Ditch

## 2 Kings 3:16

*And he said; "this is what the Lord says: Make this valley full of ditches."*

The third chapter of 2 Kings happens at the beginning of Elisha's ministry as a prophet immediately following Elijah's transport into Heaven by way of chariot. The first thing that God does through Elisha is he uses him to show the men of the city that the water in a spring nearby that was once contaminated and causing the land to be unproductive is now fresh, clean and wholesome because they poured salt into it. He tells him to share that never again will that land be unproductive. Leave it to God to heal what many say is unhealable and unproductive.

God then has Elisha tell three kings that became allies to fight against Moab to make the valley full of ditches. Why? God wanted to provide water for their livestock and for the fighting men. After they dug the ditches, the next morning water had flowed from the direction of Edom and the land was filled with water. God provided for them a stream of living water in their driest of times.

I know I have been there. I have experienced God's supernatural springs of hope, joy and peace overflowing in my life immediately following a time that I was in a spiritual drought. I have cried out to God in my desperation and quite honestly with faith probably as small as a mustard seed that God even heard me or cared to heal my hurt. He simply showed up and filled up a ditch for me to draw from.

Oh, I've dug pits before in my life. These pits were not pits that God instructed me to build. These were pits of sin and shame that I had dug with my own selfish hands. I am still in awe to this day sometimes thinking about the mercy of God towards his filth covered sinful kids like me. Some of these pits weren't even pits I had dug as a non-believer. I was following Christ when I kept chipping away at the gravel through my anxious thoughts, unbelief, fear, and insecurity. I thank God that when Jesus said "It is finished" on the cross, he meant my sins of the past, present and future. That kind of mercy is beyond my human ability to comprehend.

Yes, Jesus has pulled me out of many ditches, and He has filled up many of my dry, spiritual ditches by His loving mercy that never ends. Jesus is truly the Living Water that never runs dry in my life. When I feel dry, He quenches my spirit with His love. When I fall into another pit that I have dug, His loving arm pulls me back up on solid ground. Thanks be to God for our Savior Jesus Christ.

**Prayer focus: Talk to God about a spiritual pit you may be in, or a spiritual drought you may be feeling. Ask Him to pull you out!**

**Now that's 3:16 Power!**

# What is Your Legacy?

## 1 Chronicles 3:16

*The successors of Jehoiakim: Jehoiachin his son, and Zedekiah.*

The Bible is not only an amazing love letter written from God to us and a guidebook on how to live a fruitful, God-honoring life, it is also a detailed history book. Just nine words into 1 Chronicles 3:16 and we find ourselves knee deep into the history of three kings of Judah. These three kings took leadership and spiritual matters into their own hands by practicing idolatry, murder and many other evil practices while they held their title as king. Not one of these three kings left a legacy of love for us to emulate as modern day, believers. Johoiachin repented for his evil ways and of course our gracious God was merciful to him, but it still didn't change the fact that he suffered much tragedy in his lifetime because of his poor leadership choices and the choices of his father.

What can we learn from Johaiakim, Jehoiachin and Zedekiah? We can learn that our choices matter, our influence matters and our legacy matters, not only to us while we are alive, but to all of those who come after us for generations to come. These three kings were not only remembered for their poor behavior; it was also written in Chronicles so that it is never to be forgotten.

On the other hand, there are so many times in scripture that we read about biblical characters being honored by God because of their righteousness. There is even a Hall of Faith in Hebrews 11 that shows those dedicated believers that stood the test of time with their faith and didn't back down when faced with adversity. Just as those biblical heroes such as Noah and Abraham and Rahab are listed for their faith, many evil kings like Johoiakim, Jehoicahin and Zedekiah are mentioned for their poor choices and behavior.

What will you be remembered for? Will your legacy be one of the selfless giving of yourself to advance the gospel by loving God and loving others and making disciples? Or will your legacy be one that showed that selfish desires won out over self-control and greed won out over generosity. You see, the truth is we all are leaving some sort of legacy. What will your legacy be?

It is my heart's desire to leave a sort of chronicles myself for my children, grandchildren, and descendants. I want written in the Mydlo Chronicles names of people that we have helped as a family, names of widows that we helped support, names of orphans that we cared for, names of hungry people fed and names of lost souls won for Christ and discipled by us. I want listed in our Mydlo chronicles important family dinners celebrated, loved ones encouraged and supported, celebrations shared, and happy memories made. I want lessons that I have taught them and others, times that we have smiled and laughed together and even times that we comforted each other through trials. Yes, I think that is what I would like to see in the Mydlo chronicles.

Maybe it sounds silly, but God keeps His own chronicles; not just here, but also, in Heaven. It's the Lamb's Book of Life. It's the list of God's children who have bent a knee to the Lordship of Jesus Christ and are now sealed and redeemed for Heaven. I praise God that my name and all the Mydlo family members are written in The Lamb's Book of Life. I pray that all your family's names are as well.

So, how about you? What will your legacy be? What will be written in your family chronicles?

**Prayer focus: Spend time in prayer with God asking Him to show you how to leave a legacy of love.**

**Now that's 3:16 Power!**

## A Building Project

## 2 Chronicles 3:16

*He made interwoven chains and put them on top of the pillars. He also made a hundred pomegranates and attached them to the chains.*

2 Chronicles 3:16 focuses on King Solomon's construction of the temple in Jerusalem. King Solomon is King David's son. Solomon was given more wisdom than any other man on earth, and not only that, God decided that David would not build the temple in Jerusalem: it would be his son Solomon.

David drew up the plans for the temple. He was highly involved in the details of how the temple would be built. The details of even the pillars outside the temple were no doubt inspired by God, penned by David, but carried out by Solomon.

Has God ever called you to build something? Has He given you an idea for a ministry, a song or book, or maybe even an invention? I know He has with me. God called me to start the first MOPS (Mothers of Preschoolers) group in our town. He actually told me to do it at a stop light on my way to my mom's house. The revelation was amazing to me, I will never forget it. God said to me in His still, small, gentle voice, "Start a MOPS group." Funny thing is, I immediately said "Oh, well, thanks for thinking of me God, but I don't know how to start a MOPS group." I thought the conversation was over. It wasn't. One minute later, a MOPS commercial came on the radio. Turns out, God always wins. I went to my pastor and told him I have to obey God and start a MOPS group.

God has given me writing ideas (including this devotional), book titles and manuscripts, ministries, leaders that He wanted in place in these ministries, country songs, an invention that I have a provisional patent on, and so much more. Everything that I have ever done that has produced fruit for the Kingdom of God was not my idea, it was God's. I simply said; "Yes Lord!"

Do I think God has used me to do these things because I am someone special? Oh, HECK NO! I am a hot mess apart from Holy Spirit's leading, direction and plans. I think God wants to use all of us. The problem is we don't always hear Him correctly and sometimes we simply don't obey.

God has amazing plans for all of us. He desires to use all of us to expand His Kingdom, make disciples and lead lost souls home to Him. We simply must incline our ears to hear when He speaks and we have to do more than listen, we have to obey.

God may call you to draw up the plans for something like He did King David. Or He may call you to execute the plans like He did King Solomon. He may call you to rebuild, restore, or manage an existing plan. Whatever it is that God calls you to do; do it with courage and integrity and follow His leadership and your pillars will always stand.

**Prayer focus: Spend time in prayer with God asking Him if there is something special that He would have you do today to bring Him glory.**

**Now that's 3:16 Power!**

# Why Was I Ever Born?

## Job 3:16

*Or why was I not hidden in the ground like a stillborn child, like an infant who never saw the light of day?*

Trials and suffering can make us hit a point sometimes when we feel like lying in bed is better than getting up, staying home by ourselves and avoiding people is better than community and crying is better than laughing. Ever been there? Grief takes us there sometimes. I know all too well the pain of losing someone who you would give your life to save. The pain of losing someone we love can be so overwhelmingly excruciating that we dread the first gleam of sun each day, knowing it is a day void of our loved one.

I lost my great-niece at eighteen months old to childhood cancer. She was more like a grandchild to me. Her parents lived with us so we were a part of her everyday routine, until the day she was diagnosed and our lives were turned upside down. If you think as humans, we were made to handle these kinds of losses, you are wrong. We are not built to be able to understand or comprehend why an innocent child develops cancer, much less terminal cancer. There are no natural healing genes inside of us to overcome a loss such as this; it is simply one that we must hand over to God so He can carry it on our behalf, in order for us to carry on.

Job experienced loss upon loss in a very short time. He was at one time a very blessed and prosperous man. His farm was blessed, his family was blessed. He was financially secure and he loved God and God recognized Job as a man who honored God. Satan asked God to test him. Satan believed that Job only honored God because he was so richly blessed. He asked God to strike him with curses to see if he still would be a man that honored God. God allowed Satan to do his ugly work, as God knew Job would still honor him no matter his circumstances. But God said to Satan: "Very well, then everything he has is in your hands, but on the man himself, do not lay a finger."

Job lost his sheep and cattle and family members and his health. He lost everything dear to him but his God. Job suffered loss upon loss. Our most tragic of stories sounds like a Hallmark special compared to Job's trials and suffering. At this point in Job 3:16 we find Job wishing he had never been born. I have had these days. I have allowed the enemy of sadness to creep in, to the point where I have actually thought, "My family would probably have been better off without me." Come on my friend, I am just being real. Our feelings don't always play nice.

But God! But God always seems to dig me out of these downcast moods by one of His beautiful ways or another. He uses His Word sometimes. He uses my worship of Him sometimes. He uses prayer sometimes. He even uses hard work sometimes. Sometimes God wakes me up and tells me; "Today you need to get your hands dirty, Mo." Let me tell you, sometimes a day of serving others is exactly what we need in order to get our minds off of our problems long enough for God to comfort us and give us back our joy and our love of life. God is creative and He doesn't always use the same tactics. Sometimes we just have to sit back, be still and allow Him to show us His love.

Yes, Job was restored. He passed the test that Satan thought he would fail. In Job 1:21 we read Job saying; "Naked I came from my mother's womb, and naked I will depart. The Lord gave and the Lord has taken away; may the name of the Lord be praised." Job praised God through His trial and God brought him out. Does it say Job was never sad? No! Does it say Job never cried? No! Grief and pain are real emotions that we are all entitled to have. Job felt sadness, yet he blessed God and God delivered, restored, and redeemed him from the pit. We could all benefit by taking a lesson from Job. We need to remember that this life is filled with blessings and pain. It is simply out of obedience that we say; "Blessed be the name of the Lord."

**Prayer focus:** Today, spend some time in prayer for someone who you know of, that is going through a difficult season.

**Now that's 3:16 Power!**

# Wisdom's Benefits

## Proverbs 3:16

*Long life is in her right hand, in her left hand are riches and honor.*

I can't even fathom how many times I have said to my children; "Make wise choices." That's a mama's prayer, right? That our children think before they speak, pray before they plan and consider the consequences of their actions. We want the best for our children. We want them to prosper, be in great health, wealth and blessings and we want them to live long lives. Guess what? God our Father wants the best for us as well.

Proverbs 3:16 is talking about the benefits of wisdom: long life, riches and honor. Then yes, I will sign up for wisdom. Sounds good to me. How about you? If obtaining wisdom was just about graduating from as many degree programs as possible, at least we would know what educational track to get on and see it through to the end. But wisdom through God's eyes isn't just about education. There are so many more aspects to obtaining wisdom and the benefits from it.

Proverbs 1:7 says, "The fear of the Lord is the beginning of knowledge." Okay, so there is our starting point, fearing God. Does fearing God mean that we are shaking in our boots thinking God is going to strike us down at any second? No, fearing God means that we have a reverence for God. We have a respect and an admiration for God. We recognize our insignificance apart from God. Fearing God is about keeping Him on the throne of our hearts and never replacing Him with any other cheap substitute.

Proverbs 3 is all about getting wisdom and the benefits of obtaining it. Verse 1 starts out with God's commands and how we are to keep them in our hearts and follow them because this leads to long life. The Word then goes right into love and faithfulness. Yes, and yes. How I desire to love God and love people and remain faithful to those I love, especially to God and His plans for my life.

Verse 4 takes us into trusting God and not in our own thinking patterns. Wow, if anything screams wisdom to me, that right there does. Our thinking is jacked up without acknowledging God and His precepts all along the way. We don't think right without the Word of God. We have to renew our minds in the Word of God daily to make wise choices and keep our minds steadfast.

This proverb goes on to talk about; humility, honoring God with our wealth, accepting and trusting God's discipline in our lives, and searching for God's wisdom because it is more precious than fine gems and stones.

Yes, there are a lot of different avenues we must take to obtain wisdom, and it looks like God is at the starting gate of all of them. That is why the fear of the Lord is the beginning of wisdom.

I'm not sure how long God is talking about when He says "long life" is in wisdom's right hand and I'm not sure how much "riches and honor" God is talking about, but both of these sound pretty good to me. I've decided to enroll in God's academy of wisdom; tuition is free, and the perks are amazing.

**Prayer focus: Today, during your prayer time, ask God for wisdom in whatever area you may need His guidance in. He gives wisdom generously and to all without finding fault.**

**Now that's 3:16 Power!**

# Time and Chance Happens to Everyone

## Ecclesiastes 3:16

*And I saw something else under the sun; In the place of judgement-wickedness was there, in the places of justice-wickedness was there.*

Before I understood spiritual warfare, I thought I could out- run those creepy voices of anxiety that plagued me each day with the "what-ifs" of life. *What if I mess up? What if I let everyone down? What if something happens to my family members? What if my kids resent me? What if I am a complete failure?* Anyone else recognize this ugly voice screaming inside of you sometimes? I had grown accustomed to anxiety as an adult, since I had dealt with my overactive thinking since I was a child.

I thought I could outsmart my own fears. *If only I try really, hard to be good, these worries will go away. If only I stay involved in a lot of activities, these worries will go away. If only I pursue some sort of accomplishment or goal these worries will go away. If only I pursue pleasures, these worries will go away. If only, if only, if only.* But, they didn't.

Until I accepted Jesus Christ and began studying the Bible was I able to realize that I could live in perfect peace and I could control my thinking, my thinking didn't have to control me anymore. I had to learn how to fight the devil of my soul by memorizing, meditating on and speaking scripture out loud to renew my mind. Guess what? I experience peace every day now.

Do the worries still try to get to me? Yes, because just like this verse explains, wickedness does not discriminate. The devil loves to whisper in my ears things to attempt to steal my joy, but the difference is, now I am able to fight. I fight the good fight of faith by standing my ground against the enemy and pursuing the peace that

Christ died for, for all of us. The devil tried to steal my joy as an unbeliever, and he still tries to steal my joy as a believer. But today as a believer, I just don't let him.

I have learned how to renew my mind through replacing poor thinking patterns with the Word of God. I have learned to renew my mind through opposite action therapy by standing up to my fears so that they don't master me. I have learned how to renew my mind by saturating my life with the peace of God's precious Word so that I can speak it out loud to my flesh and to the devil so he will flee.

You know, it is possible for you to live a life worry free. Will you feel worry? Yes, most likely, but you don't have to allow worry to master you. You are free in Christ. Walk in that freedom every day and let that ugly, wicked devil know that you are done listening to his lies.

**Prayer focus: Spend time in prayer with God thanking Him that you are more than a conqueror because of Christ's sacrifice for you and thank Him that "greater is He that is in you than he that is in the world."**

**Now that's 3:16 Power!**

# If You Can't Beat Them, Don't Join Them

## Isaiah 3:16

*The Lord says "The women of Zion are haughty, walking along with outstretched necks, flirting with their eyes, strutting along with swaying hips, with ornaments jingling on their ankles"*

Is your husband pursuing holiness? It's really not my business, but it is completely your business. The best part of marriage is growing up together in our walks with Christ as a couple. I have enjoyed watching my husband become the spiritual leader of our household. He went from lost to found to completely sold out for Jesus, and there is nothing more attractive to a spouse than their partner becoming confident in Christ.

I know there are many women whose knees are just about worn out praying for their husband's salvation and walk. I know there are women who have had to take the reins as spiritual leaders in their homes because Dad is either gone from the home or simply not a Christ follower. I know there are women whose husbands have made rash, unrighteous decisions, and as mothers they have had to make difficult decisions to protect their children. I know these women are out there. I know there are women who have been abused, neglected, abandoned and more from ungodly men. I know these things because I have ministered to these women. These scenarios break my heart.

Thank God I have not only seen sad family stories. I have seen many beautiful redemption and success stories as well in the family of God. Those 50th anniversary parties and Celebration of Life events of a lifelong believer are what keep us from losing faith and believing in our abilities to overcome.

But the women of Zion were not one of those "feel good stories." The history behind this scripture Isaiah 3:16 is that the women of

Zion were the snobbish, wealthy women in Judah who were the benefactors of their husbands' crimes against the poor. These women who were adorned in tons of jewelry and expensive clothes were pretty much in today's terms wearing; "stolen bling."

Did these women steal it? Well, probably not themselves, but their husbands stole from the poor and instead of encouraging their husbands to be kind to the needy, be content and do the right thing, these ladies decided to make the best of things and bling it out.

How did God feel about this? Pretty much, how you can imagine He would feel. Isaiah 3:17 sums it up. "Therefore, the Lord will bring sores on the heads of the women of Zion; the Lord will make their scalps bald." Hmm...not going to be wearing any cute headpieces on your bald head. Not going to be feeling like anything on your head with the sores you will be nursing.

May sound harsh to you, but God is very serious about us not robbing the poor. God is close to the brokenhearted and He fights for those who are crushed in spirit. I'm going to tell you, if you are going to be ugly to the poor, you will have to deal with God. I simply love that about our protective Daddy.

What could these women have done? Just what I said earlier: encouraged their husbands to make right decisions. Yes, they may not have listened, but at least they could have tried, and if their evil husbands still decided to do evil in the eyes of God, then as wives they could have decided to not reap all of the benefits from it.

We have these choices to make daily. Do we follow the crowd, sell out and do whatever anyone else is doing because it seems to be working for them, even if it grieves our Spirit? Or do we stand up for what is right, no matter the cost, no matter the loss of material possessions, no matter the confused look from outsiders?

God is watching how we react in situations. Let's not stand and point at others living lukewarm lives and decide to let our convictions fall by the wayside as well. Let's say no to ill-gotten, dangly, bling and yes to righteousness. After all, we will see enough bling in Heaven someday. My goodness, the streets alone are made of gold!

**Prayer focus: Spend time in prayer with God and ask Him if there are any areas that you have sold out some way and let go of one of your convictions. Thank goodness, we can always repent and start over. God is good.**

**Now that's 3:16 Power!**

# You Won't Even Miss It

## Jeremiah 3:16

*"In those days, when your numbers, have increased greatly in the land," declares the Lord, "men will no longer say, "the ark of the covenant of the Lord,' it will never enter their minds or be remembered, it will not be missed, nor will another one be made."*

I am kind of a sentimental girl. I love my home. I know that my husband and I could probably sell our home and get a bigger home with more upgrades and bells and whistles for the same amount, but I have no desire to do that. I want my kids to bring their kids here. I want my future grandbabies to learn to walk in the same living room my babies learned to walk in. Well, with new flooring and different color paint, of course. Yes, this sentimental old fool likes some things to not change if I have any control over it.

At the time Jeremiah wrote this, he was talking about a huge change. The prophet Jeremiah is speaking to the remnant of Judah here. He is pleading with them to take a look at what God had already done to Israel because of their disobedience and idolatry. God allowed them to be taken captive by Assyria, and Jeremiah was trying to get Judah to repent and turn to God so that He will protect them. Judah refused and God decided to give Israel another chance. Our God is amazing with second and third and fifty- fifth chances, amen?

God pretty much let's Israel know that if they would just turn their hearts back to Him, He would give them leaders that they could trust; leaders "after His own heart". He also said; even though the Ark of the Covenant; (the holder of the ten Commandments) will be gone because of the eventual destruction of the temple, you will not miss it because I am sending something better. He is speaking of Jesus and Holy Spirit.

Yes, God is trying to let Israel know that even though the old Hebraic law that was holy and perfect and precious to them was going to be destroyed with the temple, there was coming something even better; the new covenant. The new covenant of grace. The new covenant of Jesus.

I can imagine that this would be hard for the devoted Jewish law followers to realize that something better would come along? I mean, the law is perfect. The only problem was, they weren't perfect, neither are we, and all that the law does is scream; "YOU NEED A SAVIOR".

The truth is, the New Covenant that was to come, and praise God did come, and is what we live under now, is better. It's all about Jesus, only about Jesus, always going to be about Jesus. It's not about our good works. Oh my goodness, if it were, we would all be in a mess of trouble. The New Covenant God made with His people is based on faith in Christ. That's it. We have to be obedient to the faith to stay in covenant with God.

Do you struggle with new things? I've already shared that I do. But the one thing that I have no problem accepting and even more than that, gratefully welcoming; is God's grace and mercy. I need God's grace like air. Yes, I guess I'm not so bad with change. (Well, as long as it's not my house.) Just kidding. If God calls me to anything new. I will go.

**Prayer focus: Spend time in prayer with God and ask Him if there is something new that He has for you. If so, ask Him to help you let go of the past so that you can step into your something new. You won't even miss it. I promise.**

**Now that's 3:16 Power!**

# A Mouth full of Gravel!

## Lamentations 3:16

*He has broken my teeth with gravel; he has trampled me in the dust.*

Because I have been in ministry a while, I have learned the hard way what true spiritual warfare feels like. I have described it as a roller coaster ride sometimes. It's like the feeling of that quiet, click, click, click of the upward incline that informs any roller coaster rider that a downhill is soon to be experienced, so get ready, steady your neck and hold on.

Well, that seems to be what spiritual warfare is like sometimes. We can have those quiet, peaceful moments with God, those mountaintop experiences, and those breakthroughs, but we better prepare for the inevitable kick from Satan and his ugly forces right before or right after a blessing. Why? Because it ticks the devil off to see us free and experiencing victory.

Lamentations 3:16 is no doubt one of those pre-God moment kicks, because only six verses later we read the author of Lamentations, Jeremiah, stating, "Because of the Lord's great love we are not consumed, for his compassions never fail. They are new every morning; great is your faithfulness. I say to myself, "The Lord is my portion; therefore I will wait for him." This took great faith on Jeremiah's part because this struggle he was facing was the destruction of Jerusalem by the Babylonians. Jeremiah was not being a drama king here. He was facing a battle that many of us could never even imagine.

Thankfully, Jeremiah understood spiritual warfare. He got it. He realized that though he was in an excruciating spot, one that felt like he had been dragged through gravel by the teeth, his God was faithful, and help was on the way. We only get to that kind of confidence in the middle of a trial by remembering this too shall pass and my God shall come.

How are you at remembering this when you are in a pit? How well do you continue to rejoice and worship when you are at the end of your rope and you are just about to lose grip? I know I could stand some improvement on my attitude in the middle of the storm. I'm getting better, but wow, it has taken a lot of storms to get me even here.

Have you felt like your mouth is full of gravel lately? You must remember, "He that is in you is greater than he that is in the world." (1 John 4:4) What does this mean to us? Well, this means that the God that lives on the inside of you can handle anything that ugly devil dishes out for you to face. You simply must remember to walk in your God-given authority. That is how you will learn to praise the Lord, even when you have a mouthful of gravel. You will learn to say; "The Lord is my portion: therefore I will wait for Him." Great is His faithfulness!

**Prayer focus: Spend time in prayer today asking God to give you a song in your heart, even when times are tough and you can't remember how to sing.**

**Now that's 3:16 Power!**

# Waiting on a Word

## Ezekiel 3:16

### *At the end of seven days the word of the Lord came to me:*

In the book of Ezekiel, God sent Ezekiel the prophet to speak to the exiles in Babylonia around 597 BC. God called him a "watchman" and had Ezekiel challenge the people to turn from their wicked ways of idolatry and repent. What were these seven days that are listed in Ezekiel 3:16? Well, the Word actually says that it was a time that Ezekiel sat and waited, overwhelmed. Overwhelmed and waiting on a Word from the Lord. Can you relate? I know I can.

Ezekiel knew that he had a rough road ahead of him, because God had warned him that it wouldn't be easy. God told him, "I'm sending you to an obstinate people." Well, that's comforting, right? I can imagine Ezekiel wondering, *Is there anywhere else you can send me? Anywhere at all?* God warned him of their obstinate nature, but he also told him not to worry, because he was going to be strong enough for the battle. He even says, "I made your forehead like the hardest stone, harder than flint." I have to be honest, if God told me that he was making my forehead hard like stone, I would assume there was a reason for that and I'm sure it would lead to some overwhelming feelings such as fear and anxiety. So, yes, I could relate to our precious Ezekiel's overwhelmed feeling.

Ezekiel 3:16 says, "At the end of the seven days, the word of the Lord came to me." I must tell you, I've been in a few overwhelming situations, waiting on a Word from God. I know we all have. How about some overwhelming situations like medical tests coming back? How about overwhelming situations like waiting on the divorce proceedings? How about overwhelming situations like waiting to see if an impending hurricane that is predicted to make landfall in your zip code will actually come or hopefully turn back to sea?

We have all been in overwhelming situations waiting on a word from the Lord. The question is, what does our waiting look like? When we are in a waiting pattern, are we a ball of nerves and frustration, wearing our emotions on our sleeves? Or are we an obvious Christ follower being controlled by the Holy Spirit and all of the fruits of the Spirit, patiently trusting that God will not leave us to fight alone? I think we all could honestly say, we have been in both camps. There have been situations where I have remained self-controlled and alert and not let the devil and my flesh get the best of me, and then there have been times when I have blown my witness and had to ask for forgiveness for my poor behavior or choice of words.

Ezekiel 3:16 says, "At the end of the seven days the word of the Lord came to me." I have to tell you, there's nothing like a word from the Lord. There is nothing like a comforting or even challenging word from the Lord. There is nothing like knowing that the God of the Universe has chosen to communicate with little old us. I've flown in a plane before and I always find myself thinking, *oh my goodness, we are such tiny parts of God's huge plan. But, He actually lets us be part of it.* It's overwhelming and it makes me so grateful that God takes time to speak to us, time to communicate with us, time to make us feel important.

Let me ask you this. Are you taking time to listen? We are really good at petitioning God for our needs and putting our requests out there, but we aren't always as good at waiting to hear what He has to say? When was the last time you sat quietly before the Lord and waited for a word that He had for you? I want to encourage you today to make time. Sit still and wait, and listen, because there's nothing like a word from God.

**Prayer focus: Spend time in prayer today with God simply sitting and waiting to see if He has something to say to you. He is such a gentleman and He won't yell, so make sure you are quiet. It's worth the wait.**

**Now that's 3:16 Power!**

# He's Our Defender

## Daniel 3:16

*Shadrach, Meshach and Abednego replied to him, "King Nebuchadnezzar, we do not need to defend ourselves before you in this matter.*

Have you ever felt so sure of the fact that God was going to rescue you from a situation? I have. There have been many times that I have been in situations that warranted a sort of reckless faith and abandon and I believed that no matter what, God would rescue me. This is the situation with Shadrach, Meshach and Abednego, three Jewish men who refused to bow down to King Nebuchadnezzar's statue of gold. King Nebuchadnezzar had issued a decree that every time the horns and instruments sounded in Babylon, everyone was to bow down to this statue. Well, these three brave men had made a decision out of their fear and honor of God not to take part in these practices of idolatry.

This decision could have cost Shadrach, Meshach and Abednego their lives and they knew this. When the King found out that they wouldn't bow, he had them summoned so he could question them and threaten them to do so. He told them if they didn't bow, they would be thrown into a blazing furnace. They still would not bow. Not only did they not bow, they let the King know that they were not afraid of his threats either. It appears that their trust in God's ability to defend them outweighed their fear of death.

God not only defended them when they were thrown into the fire, He marched around the fire with them, and then when the government officials went to remove them from the furnace, they came out unharmed, untouched, not even smelling of smoke. God has a way of rescuing us over and over from the fire.

Daniel 3:16 says, "Shadrach, Meshach and Abednego replied to him, 'King Nebuchadnezzar, we do not need to defend ourselves before you in this matter.' They felt it unnecessary to vindicate or defend themselves. It is unnecessary for us as well. When the flaming arrows come at us from Satan; arrows of offence or unforgiveness or lies, we do not have to be our own vindicators. We simply have to hold up our shield of faith and allow God to fight for us.

The Word tells us that He goes before us. The Lord already fought and won our spiritual battles 2000 years ago on Calvary's cross. The finished works of the cross gives us authority over anything Satan throws our way. At the name of Jesus demons have to flee, blind eyes see, the sick are made well, and the dead are raised. The blood of Jesus shed for us guarantees us ultimate victory in the end. We must remember that even though the war is already won, each battle has to be fought, (but we do not fight alone). We do not have to defend ourselves in any matter. Our God fights for us. The blood of Jesus speaks victory over any spiritual battle that we face. We simply must apply the blood when faced with each fiery dart.

The only fight that we must fight is the good fight of faith. We have to know and rely on the love of God for us. We must learn to trust that God will not only rescue us from the flames, He will march through the flames with us, and we will come out, not even smelling of smoke. To pursue the reckless faith of Shadrach, Meschach and Abednego, it is my life's goal. We do not need to defend ourselves in this matter.

**Prayer focus: Spend time in prayer with God thanking Him for being our Vindicator and Defender.**

**Now that's 3:16 Power!**

# A God of Mercy and Justice

## Nahum 3:16

*You have increased the number of your merchants till they are more than the stars of the sky, but like locusts they strip the land and then fly away.*

Let's get real for a second. Do you ever feel like every time you jump onto social media, everyone in the world has their toes in the sand except you? Do you ever get that feeling that there is a worldwide vacation going on and you are the only one who didn't get the memo? I think you know what I mean. Social media is not an accurate depiction of real life. People only show their best face, their filtered pictures and because of the beauty of technology they are able to crop out the junk that they don't want people to actually see. The truth is, no one's life is an endless vacation. The truth is good and bad, work and rest, time and chance happen to us all. For the most part, this makes sense to us, but there is just something in most of us that makes our skin crawl when we see the guilty acquitted and the unrighteous prosper. When we see evil leaders reigning and bullies triumphing over the little guys.

In the book of Nahum, this is exactly what is going on in Assyria. Assyria was the most powerful nation on earth. They were so proud of their self-sufficiency and military strength. They were plundering nations left and right and oppressing and slaughtering their victims. They were a nation of bullies and terrorists and God had put up with this long enough. He decided it was time to settle accounts, so He sent Nahum to warn the people of their impending judgment. The capital city of Assyria, Nineveh was called "City of Blood" because of their cruelty and arrogance. This is not the first time that God sent a prophet to Ninevah. Remember in Sunday school learning about our friend Jonah, who tried to avoid this dreadful city so bad that he chose the accommodations of a belly of a fish for three days instead? After Jonah's preaching in Nineveh took place, repentance took place. But years later, we see sin, idolatry, greed, and other acts of the sinful nature very much alive again in Nineveh and all of Assyria, so God sent Nahum in to pronounce God's judgement.

Nahum 3:16 says, "You have increased the number of your merchants till they are more than the stars of the sky, but like locusts they strip the land and then fly away." Allow me to translate this into Mo's country girl translation. "Hey big shot, all of your big buildings and fancy pants statues, your big old armies and bags full of cash mean nothing to me. I am God, and I've had just about enough of you." And the crowd goes wild as God settles the score. Surrounding nations that have been bullied stand to their feet in triumphal applause, noisemakers sound, horns of peace cry out in thanks and praise as our God makes all things right.

Our God is a God of order. He is a God of justice. Justice and mercy always prevail. You may be in a situation right now that seems unfair and the circumstances aren't making sense. Allow me to say to you, take heart my friend, God is watching. He is our vindicator. He is our Redeemer. Our God hates dishonest scales just like we do. Our God hates when evil is called good and good is called evil just like we do. Our God is faithful and merciful and gracious and loving and He will settle the score. You may just need to be still and wait on Him. Believe me, His timing is perfect. He will come, but not one moment too late or one moment too soon. Oh yes, friend, our God will come. Trust God. He keeps His promises.

**Prayer focus: Spend time in prayer with God and thank Him for settling the score, making all things right and for being a God of mercy and a God of justice.**

**Now that's 3:16 Power**

# Yet I Will Wait

## Habakkuk 3:16

*I heard and my heart pounded, my lips quivered at the sound; decay crept into my bones, and my legs trembled. Yet, I will wait patiently for the day of calamity to come on the nation invading us.*

God hasn't given us a spirit of fear. We know this, because God's Word tells us this. But we still fear, don't we? We still feel dread over things sometimes: am I right? Though we weren't born predisposed to be scared of anything, the truth is the world is filled with a ton of scared people desperately wanting to feel peace. I know this because I was one of them. I've written a book called "Overcoming Anxiety." I know the excruciating feeling of panic and fear. I know it all too well, so that is why I have chosen to not stay there anymore.

I have made a choice to devour the Word of God. I make it my life's ambition to continue to renew my mind in the Word of God every day and encourage others to do so through my writing and teaching. I know now the peace that passes all understanding that is promised in scripture. I have experienced this peace, and I choose daily to stay in that peace.

Habakkuk 3:16 says, "I heard and my heart pounded, my lips quivered at the sound; decay crept into my bones, and my legs trembled. Yet, I will wait patiently for the day of calamity to come on the nation invading us." Habakkuk is speaking of the Babylonian invasion. He is deciding to trust God in midst of the calamity that is happening all around him.

A word that jumped out at me when I read this scripture was the word, "yet". Yet! Yet is a word that we should all make part of our daily vocabulary.

I received a bad report at the doctors. Yet, I will take it day by day.

I know we are behind on the bills. Yet, I will continue to be faithful with our tithe.

My husband decided he doesn't want to stay married anymore. Yet, I will trust that God will take care of my children.

Yet is powerful. Yet means my circumstances don't get to determine my attitude. Yet means I know that this too shall pass. Yet means I will trust and obey, all that's real is today.

Yet gives us hope. Habakkuk's heart was pounding, his lips were quivering and his legs were trembling. Yet he trusted in The Lord. My friend, we can do the same. It is a choice. The peace that passes all understanding can guard our hearts and our minds in Christ Jesus. We simply must trust God, despite the circumstances. Because God isn't finished with us yet.

**Prayer focus: Spend time in prayer with God. Mention to Him whatever it is that you are struggling with or concerned about today. I promise you He cares.**

**Now that's 3:16 Power!**

# I Will Not Fear

## Zephaniah 3:16

*Do not fear, Zion; do not let your hands hang limp.*

Well, we found one. We found one of the 365 times in the Bible that we are commanded not to fear. Did you know that there are 365 times in the Word that say this? Do you think that this is a coincidence? It isn't. Truly, biblically, and spiritually, there are no coincidences. Our God is a detailed God. He is in all, of the details. There are 365 days in the year and there are 365 times in the Bible that we are commanded not to fear. I'm pretty sure God knew what He was doing when He breathed this detail into scripture.

Yes, we are commanded not to fear. Why do you think God had to do that? Well, just like God had to command women to submit to their husbands, God knew that our natural, imperfect nature would not do this on its own. We would have to do it on purpose. Oh yes, I submit to my husband on purpose, and I purposely do not bow down to fear.

Did I say I don't feel fear? Nope! Did I say I always feel like submitting to my husband? Nope! The truth is, our feelings a lot of the time are not on the same page as biblical truths. We have to crucify our feelings and make them submit to the Word. Our feelings do not get to dictate our actions anymore as Christians. We are people of truth and we must honor the whole truth of God.

The Word says in Zephaniah 3:16, "Do not fear, Zion; do not let your hands hang limp." Have you ever been there? Has the ugly spirit of fear ever crept in so defiantly and caused your body to react in physical ways that are uncomfortable and frightening? I know mine has. My knees can shake tremendously when fear comes over me. My hands can shake, my head can ache, my mouth can get dry and my stomach can play all sorts of tricks on me. These are physical symptoms of anxiety and fear. Do we feel them sometimes? Yes.

But, do we have to submit to their cues to run and hide? Heavens no!

The enemy will do everything in his power to get us focused on our fear and off God's perfect will for our lives of peace. It is the devil's will that we walk in fear, and it is God's will for us that we walk in perfect, flawless, fearless, peace! God speaks "Fear not" to us so many times in the Word because God knows that we need it every day. Not just every day, sometimes countless times every day, sometimes countless times every hour.

When he says, "do not let your hands hang limp" my spirit says, *take those fearful, shaking hands and lift them to Heaven in praise. Take those fearfully shaking knees and steady them under the truths of God's Word. Take that pounding heart that wants to run and hide and make it a heart sold out to stand on God's promises, no matter what!*

The truth is, it is a choice not to fear.

We can choose to FEAR NOT! We simply must make the choice, and fear not. It takes a lot of renewing our minds in the Word of God. It takes 365 times a year renewing our minds in the Word. God specifically gave us a truth for each day. Let's set our minds on them, and keep them set.

"Do not fear, my friend. Do not let your hands hang limp."

**Prayer focus: Spend time with God in prayer and hand Him whatever is bothering you today and causing fear in you. Give Him your fears and accept His peace. It is an amazing exchange.**

**Now that's 3:16 Power!**

# What Will You Be Remembered For?

## Malachi 3:16

*Then those who feared the LORD talked with each other, and the LORD listened and heard. A scroll of remembrance was written in his presence concerning those who feared the LORD and honored his name.*

Do we believe that God is paying attention and that He is keeping score? Well, I guess we shouldn't call it keeping score, but how about keeping track? This scripture lets us know that God's eyes are not absent from our day -to -day comings and goings. Malachi 3:16 says, "Then those who feared the Lord talked with each other and the Lord listened and heard." And, not only listened and heard, God wrote down some stuff.

Do you like journaling? I do. I love writing my blog and journaling in my prayer journals. I love looking back at answered prayers and fulfilled testimonies. I have greatly enjoyed filling in the blanks and writing dates and details in all four of my children's baby books and now I love writing details about their everyday lives in my blogs. Sometimes I think, *oh my poor kids, we live in such a glass house, they can't have a temper tantrum without mom using it in some object lesson when I preach.* Yes, I am one of those mamas who just loves to record details and watch how God is all over the details of life.

This scripture says to me that God is recording all of the details about His kids in His supernatural, heavenly baby books and blogs of our lives. Our God is keeping track of us, His prized possessions, His kids.

What are you going to be remembered for? If God is keeping a book of remembrance, what is He writing about you? I know what I hope He is writing about me, all the good stuff. I pray that He is one of those parents that somehow have selective amnesia about all of the nasty things that their kids did their whole lives and can't stop bragging at parties about all of their accomplishments. I pray that Father God has selective amnesia about my fears and the times that He had to comfort me over and over about the same junk. I pray that Father God has selective amnesia about my insecurities and how He would have to remind me not to point out the speck of dust in my neighbor's eye when I have a telephone pole in mine. I pray that God has selective amnesia about my faults but can't stop bragging to Jesus and The Holy Spirit and the angels just how amazing my love for Him is.

I pray that God records in His Book of Remembrance my works done in humility and the times that I truly, loved helping others. I pray that God remembers that I didn't care about money or prestige or expensive clothes ,but I cared about sharing my things with others. I pray that God remembers the times that I sacrificed and not the times when I demanded that my needs be met. Oh, I hope my baby book in Heaven is penned with God's grace and mercy.

I pray that God records in His book things that I want to be remembered for: loving God, loving people, making disciples. That's what I hope God records. That's what I want to be remembered here on earth for as well. I want to be remembered for leaving a legacy of love. How about you? What do you want God to write about you? What do you want people to say at your funeral? Come on, we all think about that sometimes, don't we? If we don't, then we should, because this life is a vapor and before we know it, we will take our last breath. What will they say about you? What do you think God will write about you?
I hope it's amazing.

**Prayer focus: Spend time in prayer with God, talking to Him about what you want to be remembered for.**

**Now that's 3:16 Power!**

# Baptism

## Matthew 3:16

*As soon as Jesus was baptized, he went up out of the water. At that moment Heaven was opened and he saw the Spirit of God descending like a dove and lighting on Him.*

Why do we get so hung up on baptism? Let's be honest, as Christians baptism can be one of those divisive issues. There are so many questions about baptism. What if I was baptized as a baby, should I be baptized now that I have given my life to Christ? Does baptism save me? What if I give my life to Christ but do not get baptized, will I go to Heaven? I hear these questions all the time in ministry.

Here is my answer. Jesus was baptized, and if you call yourself a Christian, which means "Christ follower" you need to be baptized. I don't get into doctrinal bickering with people concerning this issue because let me tell you, there are many different opinions on this. I simply say, "Follow Christ. He was baptized, so do what He did." Yes, our sweet Savior humbled Himself and made the decision to have John the Baptist baptize Him so that scripture could be fulfilled. Even John was surprised and amazed that Jesus wanted him to baptize Him. He knew who Jesus was. He knew he was baptizing the One who would divide time, the One who created everything, the One who would be our only way to Heaven. Yes, John was even amazed at the order of events, but he submitted to God's will.

We need to also submit to God's will. If baptism is a hang-up for you, please let me encourage you today. Take the plunge. Take the full plunge. Call your pastor or spiritual mentor and let them know, it is time. Your faith needs to be made public. Your relationship with Jesus needs to be displayed for all to see. Your new life in Christ needs to begin as you come up out of the water.

We make it public because Jesus made it public. When He came up out of the water, Heaven had opened and a voice from Heaven said,

"This is my Son, whom I love; with him I am well pleased." Looks like Father God was just as excited about Jesus' baptism as He was. He opened up Heaven so He could witness His son's big day. There's nothing like that feeling when our earthly father says, "I am well pleased." Oh, how I want my Heavenly Daddy to say the same thing, and it starts with obedience and ends with obedience.

What a beautiful day it was at the river Jordan the day that Jesus was immersed in baptism. What a beautiful day it is every time one of His children follow Him into the water and come out changed forevermore. Do you need to be baptized? If it was important enough for Jesus to be baptized, it's important enough for us.

**Prayer focus: Spend time in prayer with God thanking Him for the gift of baptism. Thank Him if you are baptized and thank Him if you need to be.**

**Now that's 3:16 Power!**

## Partnering in The Kingdom

## Mark 3:16

### *These are the twelve He appointed: Simon (to whom he gave the name Peter)*

Do you know that you are a co-worker with God? We are partners in the gospel with the Lord to lead the lost home. God selected his original twelve to begin the work of evangelism and every time a new believer accepts Him as Lord, the partnership grows by one. When Jesus appointed the twelve disciples imagine how powerful His plan was, considering He added one that He knew would deny Him three times, one that would betray Him into the hands of His killers, and ten others who would understand about one-third of what He would teach them and the rest would not be comprehended until He had died and resurrected. That's some dream team isn't it?

The truth is God's appointing process in choosing disciples really hasn't changed all that much since His first draft. We are all a bunch of hot messes in need of a Savior. We are all flawed and imperfect, undeserving of God's goodness but granted it because of His grace. We are all a work in progress and in need of a ton of mind renewal and flesh crucifixion.

The truth is it really is a miracle that God uses us at all. Let's be honest, our God is supernatural and He really doesn't need us, He loves us enough to allow us to partner with Him. 2 Corinthians 6:1 "As God's co-workers we urge you not to receive God's grace in vain." We are given the most precious offer from the Alpha and the Omega and that is to "Go and make disciples." We are disciple making entrepreneurs and our partner controls the stars, the moon and the ocean. Our partner created and sustains time. I'd say we partnered up.

I am convicted sometimes about keeping up my end of the partnership. God wakes me every day with breath of life. God has given me an able body, a mouth to speak and the most amazing truth to ever share. The truth that Christ came into this world to save sinners. I was once lost, but now I am found. I was once stuck in strongholds of worry and fear, but now I am at peace. I was once insecure, but now I am confident in Christ. God has given me all of this. My partner has equipped me with everything I need to hold up my end of the partnership. I simply must open my mouth, move my feet and share. How about you? Because the truth is, we all have a story to tell. We all have a part to play. God is the most amazing partner we could ever have yoked ourselves with. After all, if God be for us, who can be against us?

**Prayer Focus: Spend time in prayer with God and thank Him for allowing you to be part of His plans and purposes, then partner up!**

**Now that's 3:16 Power!**

# You Ain't Never Seen Nothing Like Him

## Luke 3:16

*John answered them all, "I baptize you with water. But one who is more powerful than I will come, the straps of whose sandals I am not worthy to untie. He will baptize you with the Holy Spirit and fire.*

John the Baptist, the man that Jesus spoke of when he said, "Of those born of women, there has not been one as great as John the Baptist." John understood humility. Listen, can you imagine being the person that Jesus would say about "there has not been one greater"? I can't even imagine. What an honor to have the King of Kings, the Messiah, the Alpha and Omega, the Creator of the Universe say of you, "not one greater." Yes, that is what Jesus said about John. Why? Why did Jesus say that about him? There are many different opinions, but since this is my book, I get to give you mine. I believe Jesus was speaking in such reverence of John, not because of John's human attributes. God is no respecter of persons. I believe Jesus was referring to John's spirit. You see, never before the birth of John in scripture do we read about someone born with The Holy Spirit. John the Baptist was born with The Holy Spirit. My heart says that's what Jesus was referring to. Listen mamas, I know you think your child is gifted, but that baby still needs to accept Christ someday to be filled with the Spirit. Not John though, he was born with The Holy Spirit. I believe that's what set him apart from other humans.

Jesus honored John, but John's humility (which probably came from the Spirit) was strong enough in him to realize, I may be a prophet, I may be baptizing, but my whole life was created to be a voice speaking of the One coming shortly after me. John knew who he was, but more than that, he knew whose he was. John's humility allowed Christ's light to shine. Luke 3:16 says, "John answered all, 'I baptize you with water. But one who is more powerful than I will come, the straps of whose sandals I am not worthy to untie. He will baptize you with The Holy Spirit and fire.' In other areas John is ministering and Jesus comes towards him and John says, "Behold, the Lamb of God, who takes away the sins of the world." John was taken aback when Jesus would even step on the scene. He would say things like, "I must become less, He must become more."

Friend, our hearts must reach the humility level of John's to be used in a way that John was able to be used for the Kingdom. Our lives need to be constantly portraying, "less of me, more of Jesus." God's Word tells us to humble ourselves under God's mighty hand so that in due time, He will lift us up. Oh, friend, what an honor to be lifted up by God, according to His timeline, which is perfect. We need to realize in a world of self-promotion, that God's promoting power is lasting, ours is temporary. If we exalt ourselves, it won't last. Lifting yourself up requires holding yourself up and that sounds exhausting to me. How about you?

John knew to say, "Please, don't look at me, look at Him." Oh friend, if we can do that with our lives. If our lives can be lived with the mission to glorify God in every area, reflect Him to society and shine His light instead of our own, we can truly be powerful. We can truly be ambassadors for Christ and partners in The Kingdom. John was used by God to speak of something better coming. Guess what? That's our calling as well. You see, Jesus is coming back. He's not coming as a baby next time, He is coming as King. It is our job today, just like it was John's, to say, "Behold the Lamb of God who takes away the sins of the world." It's our job to say, "I must become less, He must become more." It is our job to say, "Oh, you just wait until you see the One coming." We are modern day John the Baptists. We may not have been born with the Holy Spirit, but if we have accepted Christ, we carry Him now.

Today, what can you do to let the world know, the One is coming? Because they ain't never seen nothing like Him. (Mo's country girl translation)

**Prayer focus: Spend time in prayer with God asking Him how you can become less, and He can become more in your life.**

**Now that's 3:16 Power!**

# The Giver

## John 3:16

*For God so loved the world that He gave His one and only Son, that whoever believes in Him shall not perish but have eternal life.*

Life has been crazy lately. Not bad crazy, just busy crazy. My oldest son got his first apartment the week after Christmas, so we moved him in, while at the same time my other son and his wife bought their first home so we helped them paint and move. Here at our house, along with working full time in the ministry, we have been cleaning and packing up Christmas, and preparing to host a family of five from out of state at our home for two nights. It has been a painting and sorting and organizing hurricane at the house for two weeks straight. Did I mention it was the two weeks right after the December Christmas craziness?

Well, I hit a wall yesterday. I hit the to-do list wall. I hit the, "who wants something from me now? I want normal life back," wall. I know when I'm hitting my "giving too much and not resting enough," wall when I am annoyed with how naturally nice my husband is, when I have to truly "put on" nice like a garment. When I see my husband look at me with those scared eyes and I know he's thinking, *Did she not have her coffee today*? I knew it was time to slow down.

You see, when I don't give myself a stop button, I give and give until my giving is laced with bitterness. I work full time in the ministry and ministry literally has no stop button. The needs never stop so, those in ministry have to set good boundaries or we hit these walls some days. Now when the needs of ministry match the needs at home, and I don't unwind properly, it gets ugly.

Thank God today I had on the schedule to get coffee with my two friends at Cracker Barrel. We try to get together once a month or every other month just to talk, relax and laugh. Wow, did I need that. I came home after breakfast, sat down to pray and first thing I felt led to do was repent. I had to apologize to God for my lack of boundaries. I had to ask God for forgiveness for my bad attitude. I had to repent for my complaining that I found myself doing. As I sat and looked out the window praying, I felt God say, "I love you, Mo."

I'm not kidding you, I felt Him say, "I love you." It caught me off guard like God's crazy, amazing unconditional love does sometimes. I thought, "Really God? You love me even when I'm this much of a mess? You love me even when all my flesh wants to do is forget about any responsibilities and just go lay on a beach somewhere lathered in suntan oil and nap until sundown? You still love me when I'm a brat?" But the truth is, yes, He does.

God loves us so much. He can't help Himself from loving us. He loves us on our good days. He loves us on our bad days. He loves us when we are serving and He loves us when we need to relax and receive. He loves us beyond any natural explanation of love. He is relentless about His love and His love is unconditional and spectacular.

God's perfect love heals us. God's perfect love redeems us. God's perfect love restores us. God's perfect love casts out fear. God's perfect love saves us! God's perfect love is why He sent His most precious treasure, His son, to stand in the gap for our sins. God sacrificed His most marvelous masterpiece, Jesus to remind us that no matter what a mess we are, He loves us more.

You know, I kept thinking I was doing so much giving, but after giving everything I had to create a nice Christmas for my family and a wonderful Christmas season for my staff and volunteers and then giving my time, talent and energy on all of these home projects, today I was reminded who the real giver is. The real Giver is our heavenly Father. The truth is you can't out give God. Don't ever even try.

We give God our mess. He gives us a message.

We give God our tears. He gives us His treasures.

We give God our hurts. He gives us His healing.

We give God our junk. He gave us His Jesus.

You know, God truly gave Jesus to us out of love. That kind of love, I believe we will only be able to understand fully when we are with Him face to face someday in glory. "For God so loved the world that He gave His one and only Son, that whoever believes in Him will not perish but have eternal life." I love that word "whoever" in there. Whoever means whoever. God is no respecter of persons. God doesn't just give the gift of eternal life to those who never throw pity parties for themselves. God doesn't just give the gift to those people who act like they have it all together. God doesn't just give the gift to those people who deserve it. Because, ya'll, if this was the case, no one would receive it, would we? Can I get a witness?

God gives the gift of eternal life to whoever would believe in His precious Son. God puts all of His eggs in the Jesus basket. God is pretty, serious about us knowing His perfect Son intimately. Our eternal home in Heaven is secure someday because of our faith and belief in His One and only Son. Whoever believes in Jesus gets the gift.

Yes, our God is a giver. You just can't out give God. This whoever is done trying. I am thankful for the gift. Yes Lord, I receive it, in Jesus' Name. Have you received it? If not, today is the day. Bow a knee to Jesus today. God's gift of eternal life is free, but it wasn't cheap. It cost Him everything. It cost Him His Son. Trust in Jesus today. If you have never made Him Lord, don't wait. Open the gift of Jesus. It's packed with eternal power.

**Prayer Focus: Ask God to forgive you for your sins. Let God know that you believe Jesus died on the cross and rose again for you. Ask Jesus to come into your heart so that you can follow Him for the rest of your life. Say out loud: Jesus is Lord!**

**Now that's 3:16 Power!**

# Faith in The Name

## Acts 3:16

*By faith and in the Name of Jesus, this man whom you see and know was made strong. It is Jesus' name and the faith that comes through Him that has completely healed him, as you can see.*

Here we find the two apostles John and Peter heading to the temple to pray when they find a familiar sight. It was a man that they recognized who was lame and was begging for money like he had for years. He had his hand held out ready to receive any sort of gift anyone could give him that would help him find enough food for the day or perhaps enough money for lodging that night. But this day he received more than he had ever expected. This day he encountered the Bread of Life and The Living Water of Jesus Christ. On this day, his hand was not filled with coins. He was given so much more. He was given a chance at life.

Peter looked right at the man and said to him these precious words, "Silver and gold I do not have, but what I do have, I give you. In the Name of Jesus Christ of Nazareth, walk." Peter took the man by the right hand, helped him up and the man instantly began to walk. This man received his miracle that day at the temple gate called Beautiful.

That day the disciples walked in the authority of the Name of Jesus and this man became healed. Well, as usual, as soon as any supernatural miracle or work of God happens, the people try to figure it out or reason, how this must have happened. The people begin looking at Peter and John like they were superhuman. Peter recognizes this and rebuked them and reminded them that this power that was used to heal this man, was not from them, it was Jesus in them. It was complete faith in the Name of Jesus that made this man who was lame from birth, literally jump around in amazement and thanks.

Acts 3:16 reads, "By faith in the Name of Jesus, this man whom you see and know was made strong. It is Jesus' name and the faith that comes through him that has completely healed him, as you all can see." My friends, it is imperative that we remember the truth of this scripture each day that we fulfill the great commission to go into the world and make disciples of all nations. We must remember it while we are serving in our ministry of reconciliation that we have all been given. We must remember this while we are walking in the fruits of the Spirit and the five-fold ministry gifts God has given us. We must remember who it is that is actually doing the miracles that we are blessed to see each day. We must remember that it is only because of the precious name of Jesus Christ on our lips and the amazing Holy Spirit residing on the inside of us that we are able to do anything. We better be sure to remain humble and never mistake the gifts with the giver of the gifts.

The name of Jesus on our lips is powerful. The name of Jesus is stronger than any mental stronghold, habit, or hang-up. The name of Jesus is more powerful than any storm that may have blown into our lives. The name of Jesus is more effective than any three-part plan or strategy we can concoct on our best of days. The name of Jesus is where our power comes from. We simply cannot forget where our power is found. Our authority is blood bought and able to conquer always because of and only because of The name of Jesus Christ. The name that is above all names should be continually on our lips, and constantly where we place our trust.

**Prayer focus: Spend time in prayer thanking God for the precious name of Jesus, the name that is above all names.**

**Now that's 3:16 Power!**

# Ruin and Misery

## Romans 3:16

### *ruin and misery mark their ways*

To understand why today's devotional opens up with "ruin and misery mark their ways" we have to dig into the scriptures that it immediately follows. I mean, have you ever played "Bible roulette? Oh, yes, we have all done it. Bible roulette is usually played when we are in sort of a spiritual lazy mood. We ask God a question then we say, "Okay God, wherever I open this bible, please give me your answer." Bible roulette can freak you out quite honestly. Does God sometimes play along with us? Oh yes, when we are babies, but I believe that once we grow up a little in our faith, God expects us to study and diligently attempt to understand the history, meaning and application of each scripture He carefully placed in His Word. Yes, God may sometimes throw us that little spiritual bone, occasionally, but most of the time, we need to study it out.

Romans 3:16 is describing the plight of someone who tries to pursue righteousness apart from the grace of God, simply by trying to follow the works of the Old Covenant Law. Romans 3:10 says, "There is no one righteous, not even one." This scripture is explaining that it does not matter whether you are a Jew or a gentile, your righteousness does not come from your own good works. You are a sinner, we all are. Our righteousness comes when we accept the sacrifice of Jesus Christ and what He did for us on the cross, and when we make Him Lord of our lives, we are given His righteousness. There is nothing we have ever done or can do to make ourselves righteous, only Jesus makes us righteous. We are the righteousness of God in Christ Jesus, period.

The Apostle Paul is trying to get his point across that we are not saved through works, it is by grace we have been saved, through faith in Jesus and there's no other way to stand in front of a Holy God someday if not covered by the precious blood of Jesus Christ.

Oh, the wonderful blood of Jesus is the only thing that can wash away the sins of our past, our present and our future. The blood that Jesus shed for us allows us to be clothed in robes of righteousness, washed, clean and new. Why in the world would we try to work to earn a salvation that is already so freely given to us by our merciful Savior Jesus?

Oh friend, we still try. We still try to work and work to prove to ourselves and to others that we are worthy of God's love and forgiveness, but we need a fresh revelation today that by doing so, ruin and misery mark our way. Why not today accept the gift of God's forgiveness, His righteousness, and His deliverance that is truly already ours when we have surrendered to Jesus? Why not today walk in perfect peace knowing that Jesus' blood paid it all? It truly was all the sacrifice needed, for all of us, once and for all.

**Prayer focus: Spend some time praying to God and thanking Him for the precious blood of Jesus. Thank God that you are the righteousness of God in Christ Jesus.**

**Now that's 3:16 Power!**

# Temple or Trash Dump?

## 1 Corinthians 3:16

*Don't you know that you yourselves are God's temple and that God dwells in your midst?*

Can you relate to that dreaded afternoon decision: cookies with my coffee today or a banana? It truly is a choice that we must purposely make isn't it? But, that's not the only one that we will make each day. Let's think about a few decisions we make each day, that affect our health and how we treat our bodies. Or should I say, how we treat our temples? Before I go any further, keep in mind that this girlfriend is right in it with you. I soar somedays and I fail somedays.

Coffee and a muffin for breakfast **OR** black tea and an egg and fruit?

Take the dog for a walk for a half hour **OR** get right in the shower and skip exercise?

Clean the house with natural cleaners **OR** grab the cheap ones, not even looking at ingredients?

Make a menu for the week so you cook healthier meals at home **OR** just play it by ear each day and sometimes just grab drive-thru since it's easier?

Spend time in God's Word each morning and in prayer and meditation **OR** save the bible studying for the Pastor and just wait until Sunday to see what he has to say?

Take the stairs at work **OR** wait in line for the elevator?

Watch your afternoon caffeine so that you go to bed on time and get 8 hours of sleep that night **OR** just run through the drive through again for your grande', mocha, double latte, espresso, whatever so you have energy enough just to get through the afternoon, and worry about the later sleep effects, later?

Come on friend, we make these decisions almost every day, don't we? These are only a small list of the important decisions we make whether or not to care for our own health. Most of us have developed excuses for those times that we make the wrong choices. I know I have. But the truth is we aren't hurting anyone but ourselves. We justify our choices saying, "It's my body, I can treat it how I choose." But, is it? Is it our bodies? The Word of God actually says that our bodies don't belong to us, they belong to God.

The Word says in 1 Corinthians 6:19-20 says, "Do you not know that your bodies are the temples of the Holy Spirit who is in you, whom you have received from God? You are not your own; you were bought at a price; therefore, honor God with your bodies."

The Word here tells us that God owns our body. Our body belongs to Him. When God sent His precious Holy Spirit to dwell on the inside of us when we became born again after making Jesus Lord, our bodies became God's temple. The Holy Spirit resides on the inside of us. 1 Corinthians 3:16 says, "Don't you know that you yourselves are God's temple and that God dwells in your midst?"

Let me ask you, do you feel like you must respect your church when you walk into it because it is God's house? I hope so. Well, your body is God's house as well. The Holy Spirit lives inside of believers. We carry Christ. We are not only bodies, we are temples, and temples are Holy ground and should be treated as such. Quite honestly, a lot of us treat our bodies like trash dumps instead of temples most of the time. We eat what we should not, we fail to exercise like we should, we don't get enough sleep and we watch garbage on TV and in movies that poisons our souls. Unfortunately, we all fall short in this area from time to time. Thank God for the grace of God which leads us to repentance.

We need to repent for treating our temples poorly and we need to make some diligent efforts to treat our bodies like holy temples set apart and consecrated as a living sacrifice unto our Lord. After all, the longer we live, the more time we have, to share Christ with a lost world. We are called to represent Christ in this world. The longer we live, the longer we represent.

Will you join me in minute by minute, hour by hour, day by day, making more of an effort? I know that we can all become more aware of our decisions and work at making better ones. I'm starting right now. I am going to choose to not go and eat that piece of chocolate that is in my fridge that's been calling my name the whole time I've been typing. Help me, Jesus.

**Prayer focus: Spend time in prayer with God and ask Him what areas you can work on to take better care of His temple, your body.**

**Now that's 3:16 Power!**

**I Can See!**

**2 Corinthians 3:16**

*But whenever anyone turns to the Lord, the veil is taken away.*

I love those cool pictures that have other hidden objects in them. You just have to keep looking until your brain will actually let you see it. It always amazes me when I can finally see the hidden object. It is almost like there is a veil over the object until our brain says, "Okay I'm going to pull the veil away in one, two, three and you will see it."

When Moses came down from Mount Sinai with the Ten Commandments his face was glowing after being in the presence of God. The glory of God was covering him so intensely that the people were terrified by the brightness of his face. Moses would go and talk to God, then have to cover his face with a veil when he would return to speak with the Israelites. This prevented the people from seeing God's glory fade away from him. The apostle Paul later taught that the veil also represents people struggling to see and understand Christ's true nature and His love for them.

The good news is, when people choose to accept Christ, the veil is removed. There is so much significance in this scripture, "But whenever anyone turns to the Lord, the veil is taken away." With the veil taken away, we can approach and communicate and be in relationship with a holy and perfect God. With the veil taken away, we can see the sin in our lives that we may now break free from once and for all. With the veil taken away, we can experience the freedom and joy that comes with the ministry of the Holy Spirit. With the veil taken away we can not only see God's glory manifest in our lives, we are able to glorify God in all that we do and say.

When Jesus died on the cross, took His last breath, and said, "It is finished," the veil to the Holy of Holies tore in two. No longer would only the High Priest be able to approach the throne room of God on behalf of us. Since that glorious moment, God made a way for all mankind to be able to boldly come before The Father at any time, night or day, because our High Priest Jesus has made the way for us. It is God's will that all people enter into a personal love relationship with Him. We can do this because of Jesus, the blood He shed and the veil that was torn.

What veils are you still holding up spiritually and not allowing God to shine His glory upon? What areas are you still hiding from God, like the Israelites who were frightened by the light of God's glory? May I encourage you today to let God's light shine brightly in any dark areas you are experiencing? Allow your man-made veil to be torn in two so that His light may overpower the darkness. The Holy Spirit is the light, and where the Spirit of the Lord is, there is freedom.

**Prayer Focus: Spend time in prayer with God asking Him to show you where you may still be veiling yourself from His glory. Allow His light and love to overpower you and shine light into any dark areas in your life. Shine with Him!**

**Now that's 3:16 Power!**

# The Promised Seed

## Galatians 3:16

*The Promises were spoken to Abraham and to his seed. The Scripture does not say "and to seeds", meaning many people, but "and to your seed," meaning one person who is Christ.*

Have you ever watched an addict, who finally was able to break free from the destructive powers of drugs, return to their drug use? Have you ever witnessed an obese person, who has worked extremely hard to lose the weight, return to their poor eating habits and regain the weight? I have witnessed both difficult situations. Quite honestly the best part of full- time ministry is seeing God change people's lives. The hardest part of ministry is seeing people self-sabotage themselves and return to their hurts and habits.

This is exactly what was happening in the Galatian church. The Apostle Paul was extremely frustrated watching Jewish believers who had received salvation the only possible way, by grace through faith, return to attempting to follow the old Jewish laws. The Jewish Christians were returning to their bondage. They were feeling like they needed to earn their salvation that cannot be earned; it comes by faith, through grace.

Paul asks them in Galatians 3:16, "Who bewitched you?" He goes on to ask them, "Did you receive the Spirit of God by doing anything?" The answer is no. They received the precious Holy Spirit the same way that we do, by grace through faith in Jesus Christ, period. Jesus is the only way to Heaven. Jesus is the Promised Seed. The Seed that was promised to Abraham's descendants even before Abraham existed.

In Genesis 3:15 the Word says, "And I will put enmity between you and the woman, and between your offspring (seed) and hers: he will crush your head and you will strike his heel." The part that says, "he will crush your head" is the foreshadowing of Satan's demise when

Jesus raises from the dead. Looks like Jesus has always been Father God's plan.

Paul had to rebuke the Galatians and encourage them to knock off the insane thinking that they could do anything righteous on their own. They needed to remember that Christ died to set them free. They simply had to begin to walk in that freedom that was already theirs, and so do we.

Christ died for you so that you may live a life of freedom. Don't go back to trying to live this life on your own. What areas in your life are you trying to "fix yourself"?

Christ died for you. Whatever deliverance you need or stronghold you are struggling to break free from, you can be set free by the promise, not the law. The Promised Holy Spirit that lives on the inside of you as a Christ follower, is how you will remain free.

The promise, not the law, keeps you from returning to the cookie jar.

The promise, not the law, keeps you from returning to the pills.

The promise, not the law, keeps you from straying in your marriage.

The promise, not the law, keeps you from yelling when you want to act calmly.

The promise, not the law, keeps you from anxiety and fear.

It is the promised Holy Spirit that only is made available to us because of the promised Seed, Jesus Christ that has set us free from the bondage of sin. It is through that promised Seed that we remain free. Oh friend, who has bewitched you? You are free! Now walk in that freedom.

**Prayer focus: Spend time in prayer with God thanking Him for your freedom that comes from nothing that you did, but everything that He did.**

**Now that's 3:16 Power!**

# Power is Available to Us

## Ephesians 3:16

*I pray that out of his glorious riches he may strengthen you with power through his Spirit in your inner being*

What a beautiful prayer the Apostle Paul prayed for the Ephesian church and for us. His prayer that he prayed for us is a prayer for strength and power. Could you use some strength and power? When I scroll through social media, I am reminded that we all could use a little strength and power. I see people posting about their ailments, their struggles, and their weaknesses. I see people mentioning the cookies that they are having a hard time saying no to. Oh wait, that was my post yesterday.

The truth is, we all could use a little supernatural power to live fearlessly in this fallen world. Every day, we lose loved ones, our bodies get sick, our finances fall through, and our kids sometimes act crazy. We get caught up in addictions and strongholds of the enemy, and we need some power to break free. Thank God that we have the Holy Spirit.

When I think back to my life before I had made Jesus Lord, it was a life of powerlessness and discontentment. I was always searching for something to fill that void that only Christ could fill. We all do it. We try to fill ourselves up with material goods, treasures, that "one person" we think will complete us, food, exercise, you name it. Before we have the indwelling Holy Spirit, it is like we are driving in a car that just can't ever get the gas tank up over a quarter of a tank. It just seems to keep running dry.

I personally was an anxious, fearful, insecure mess. I was always caught in the comparison trap with others. I thought I had to compete with other women to hold on to my husband. I strived to be the perfect wife, the perfect mother, the perfect homemaker, but

I always seemed to fall short. I was like a person out in the ocean of life, just treading and treading, but sinking quicker than I could swim.

But God! God rescued me. He saved me and He filled me with supernatural power through the precious Holy Spirit. He planted His Spirit on the inside of me and He gave me His Word, and my life has never been the same. Oh, thank you Jesus it has never been the same.

The Holy Spirit has healed hurts in me that were so deep I didn't even know they existed. The Holy Spirit has taught me how to understand the Word of God that has renewed my mind and continues to renew my mind each day. The Holy Spirit has healed my anxiety by teaching me how to trust God. The Holy Spirit has given me a powerful love for others in replacement for my competition with others. The Holy Spirit is powerful. The Holy Spirit's power made manifest in my life and in the lives of all who call on the name of Jesus is exactly what Paul prayed for. I thank God Paul prayed that prayer for me. How about you?

**Prayer focus: Spend some time in prayer with God thanking Him for the power of the Holy Spirit at work in those who believe.**

**Now that's 3:16 Power!**

# I Should Know This by Now

## Philippians 3:16
*Only let us live up to what we have already attained.*

Watching my husband work on tasks around our house and store is almost amazing to me sometimes. He is what people would call a "jack -of- all -trades." He knows how to clean the dryer vent, change the oil in the lawn mower, put new chains on the kids' bikes, and replace ballasts on the lights at the store, all while he's on the phone closing real estate deals to support our family.

When stuff comes into the resale shop that many people have just donated because they don't know how to fix something, Tommy will do his magic and the next thing we know it's on the showroom floor for sale to support the ministry. Has Tommy always known how to do all of these things? Heavens, no! He's learned all of these things in good ole "on the job training" in life and ministry.

When we were first married, he and I didn't know how to do very many handy things at all. We both had to learn through education and trial and error. Thank God for godly mentors in the faith and in life.

The Apostle Paul says, "Only let us live up to what we have already attained." It brings me great peace to know that God is not going to expect us to be excellent at things we haven't learned yet. He teaches us new things each day and gives us grace and mercy as we learn and improve upon them.

God does expect us to live out obediently the lessons we've already learned though. He expects us to grow. He expects us to improve. He expects us to live up to what we have already attained.

In what areas have you already received the lesson and training but are struggling to put into practice the things you've learned? Let's make an effort together to keep striving to get better and better each day, growing in the gifting and grace from our Lord Jesus Christ. The truth is, we should be growing and improving and learning right up until the day that we take our last breath. If we are still here, God still has something new for us to learn.

My Tommy is a pretty, handy guy to have around. I think I'll keep him.

**Prayer Focus: Spend time in prayer with the Lord asking Him to teach you some new lessons as you work obediently on the lessons you've already learned.**

**Now that's 3:16 Power!**

## Lifting the Name of Jesus High and Renewing our Minds in the Word

### Colossians 3:16

*Let the message of Christ dwell among your richly as you teach and admonish one another with all wisdom through psalms, hymns, and songs from the Spirit, singing to God with gratitude in your hearts.*

Once a month Unforsaken Women Corporation hosts an interdenominational, community -wide Bible study and women's event where the Name of Jesus is lifted high and women are taught how to renew their minds in the Word of God. That is our mission statement. I feel like I could say that mission statement in my sleep. I have written it so many times on grant requests, invitations, event promotions and more. Hosting a monthly women's event for women from all different denominations and churches has been one of the joys of my heart for the past 6 years now.

Yes, for six, almost seven years, a group of ladies and my husband and myself have set an agenda, invited the community, set out chairs and equipment, prepared food and delivered a message to set the stage for the Holy Spirit to do what only He can do, and for six years, almost seven, God has blessed it.

We average about forty to fifty women. These women come out to a meeting center on a Tuesday night, after long days dealing with work, raising kids, taking care of homes and life in general. They could just stay home and rest, but they don't.  These women come ready to receive a Word from God and ready to lift Jesus' name in worship. These women come hungry, and I pray they leave full.

Our leaders have set up and torn down our equipment more than 70 times now. Why? Because it is God's will that we let the message of Christ dwell in us richly. It is God's will that we teach the Word of God. It is God's will that we admonish each other through psalms, hymns, songs of the Spirit with thankful hearts. We set it up, we put it on and we do this every month for free for our community because it's a Holy Spirit thing and where the Spirit of the Lord is, there is freedom.

Unforsaken Women supports women and children locally and globally. We have our once a month women's event, a resale shop to support our mission where we also have our food pantry, a single moms ministry, a widow support group and a school in Haiti that we support where over 150 kids get a Christian education because of people like the ladies at Unforsaken Women. We have television segments where we teach the Word of God through practical life lessons and devotionals. It's an absolute privilege to serve with the leadership team of Unforsaken Women as we let the world know about the One True Way to Heaven, Jesus Christ.

Colossians 3:16 is one of my favorite scriptures. It reminds me of Unforsaken Women. It makes me smile to know obedience to scriptures such as this is NOT a burden. It is a true joy indeed. I love the Word. I love Worship. I love our Jesus. Don't you?

**Prayer focus: Spend time with the Lord today asking Him how you can allow the message of Christ to dwell in you richly.**

**Now that's 3:16 Power!**

## Where Does Your Peace Come from?
## 2 Thessalonians 3:16 NIV

*Now may the Lord of peace himself give you peace at all times and in every way. The Lord be with all of you.*

I fell for it again. I got swept away in a crazy mental distraction today. I had an idea to sell our house and buy or build a home in the country so that our son Eli can have a horse. Did we sell? Oh goodness, no. I love my home. I simply wasted an afternoon that my husband could have been working on other real estate deals, and I could have been studying and writing just so we could drive out to a really old rickety log home on 3 acres, "just to see it."

My sweet husband is never too busy to entertain my spontaneous whims. I think he knows it is not worth his breath and that my Holy Spirit will remind me quicker than he can, how blessed and content I am in the home we have now. Sometimes it takes an hour out of his day and a drive through for some afternoon coffee, but my ADD usually subsides quickly.

It is almost amazing to me that I can get so distracted from my business at hand so easily. It is no doubt at the hand of the enemy. I am quite sure I'm not alone in this. I think Americans, in general, struggle finding contentment and peace and letting go of always having to be striving for more. Whether it's material goods, thinking we need to improve our looks, growing our wardrobe or even staying faithful in relationships. Something in our selfish nature always says, "but, just one more thing."

2 Thessalonians 3:16 reminds us that it is the Lord of peace who gives us peace. Our peace does not come from adding one more flower to our garden, one more dress to our wardrobe, that new job, a different boss, or that new man. These things will always leave us wanting for more. True contentment, true peace, true joy, comes only from the Lord of peace. We must seek Him in prayer and in His Word and ask God to reveal to us the distractions and cravings that

are keeping us from His perfect peace. We must sacrifice those things on the altar of our hearts and put The Lord of Peace back on His throne where He belongs.

So, no, we did not buy the log cabin. It was actually yucky. I came home to my beautiful, clean home and I sat down on my 15- year-old prayer swing on my back porch and I thanked the Lord of peace for reminding me how blessed I am. Hey, but it made for a great devotional!

**Prayer focus: Spend time in prayer with God asking Him to show you where you may be seeking for peace apart from your relationship with Him.**

**Now that's 3:16 Power!**

# Mysteries
## 1 Timothy 3:16 NIV

*Beyond all question, the mystery from which true godliness springs is great: He appeared in the flesh, was vindicated by the Spirit, was seen by angels, was preached among the nations, was believed on in the world, was taken up in glory.*

We can get so confused about so many things. We can overthink everything to the maximum levels sometimes. "Which came first, the chicken or the egg?" "Is there truly someone for everyone, and maybe we just mess it up and miss it sometimes?" "Why did God make skunks anyways, do they actually have a purpose?" There literally are mysteries that we may never have the answer to here on earth. Quite honesty, when we get to Heaven, I doubt we will even care about asking God these questions as we will be so happy and content there.

There are mysteries though that the Bible solves for us if we simply will dig in and study to find ourselves approved as workmen who correctly handle the Word of Truth. Here is an example of a solved mystery, the mystery of godliness. If we wonder, how can we walk in the ways of godliness and live like Christ in this difficult world, the answer is, we must understand Who Christ is, in order to live like Him.

"Beyond all question, the mystery from which true godliness springs is great: He appeared in the flesh, was vindicated by the Spirit, was seen by angels, was preached among the nations, was believed on in the world, was taken up in glory."

Here are the Cliff's notes on this scripture: Christ took off His priestly robes in Heaven to put on skin, to live like us. The Holy Spirit is in Christ which allowed Him to resurrect from the dead. The world saw Him and the message of the gospel began to be preached. The Words "was taken up in glory" prove that Jesus was not simply a man who rose from the dead. He is divine. He is Lord.

Once we can truly, understand Christ, we can begin to live like Christ, which is how we will live a godly life. We study Christ by studying His Word. Jesus is The Word made flesh. He is exactly like the Word. So, if we want to live like Christ, we must live according to the Word.

Yes, this mystery of godliness is really no mystery at all. It is recorded for us to study. We simply must open His Word, study it, and put it into practice. Remember, we cannot just study it, we must live it. Mystery solved.

**Prayer focus: Spend time in prayer with God asking Him for the diligence you need to study His Word so that you can begin to live like the Word Made Flesh, Jesus.**

**Now that's 3:16 Power!**

# All Sorts of Cleaning Tools

## 2 Timothy 3:16

*All Scripture is God-breathed and is useful for teaching, rebuking, correcting and training in righteousness.*

I had just finished my afternoon coffee, or as I like to call it, "my round two fuel". I decided to head out back and work on the porch, garden and pool a few minutes. If you are a homeowner, you know that housework is never done. When we spend a whole day working outside, the inside looks neglected. If we obsess about the inside, we look outside and there are weeds growing in the marigolds. I don't mind it though. I enjoy housework. I call it "job security" as a homemaker, wife, and mother.

I weeded the garden a little and skimmed the pool, then I went in on my screened- in porch to sweep. I absolutely love the potted plants on my porch. I just have to consistently sweep up any dead, already budded flowers that have landed outside the pots. Sometimes it's actually pretty, with all the petals on the floor it looks like someone just got married out back. Well, that's kind of stretching it a bit.

As I was sweeping, I thanked God for my broom. I know you are probably thinking, "Well, that's kind of a weird thing to be thankful for." I really am thankful for my broom though. I vacuum the back porch a lot, but when I am cleaning up the dead leaves and buds, it requires a broom to get into the hard to reach spots. The vacuum works for jobs it is designed for, and the broom works well for things it is designed for.

This spoke to me about the Word of God. 1 Timothy 3:16 says, "All scripture is God-breathed and is useful for teaching, rebuking, correcting and training in righteousness." I thought, "Yes Lord, all of Your Word works differently for different tasks."

God's Word is entirely just that, the very words of God. God spoke it to men to put in writing as it was carried along by the Holy Spirit. The

Old Testament and the New Testament are both equally as important to read, study, meditate on and apply it to everyday life. The Proverbs and the Psalms are just as important as the gospels and Genesis is just as important as Revelation.

God uses all His Word to teach us. God uses all His Word to rebuke and correct us when we need discipline and God uses all His Word to train us to be righteous. He does not pick and choose different areas of the Bible to call more important and use to implement His plans and purposes. God is too creative and detailed and amazing for that.

The truth is, if we tried to clean our entire home inside and out with just a mop, we would struggle. That sounds silly to even say I know, but the truth is we do this in our Christian walk. We memorize one or two scriptures and think that those two verses are enough to help us walk in victory as a Christian, and then we wonder why we are struggling to find peace.

I love verses like Jeremiah 29:11, "For I know the plans I have for you says The Lord, plans to prosper you and not to harm you, plans to give you hope and a future," but that verse doesn't help me when I get into fear. I need scriptures combatting fear to fight the enemy of fear in my life. I love scriptures like 1 John 4:8, "Perfect Love casts out fear," but that scripture doesn't help me when I am trying to seek God's purpose for my life. I would need to run back to Jeremiah 29:11 for that.

Hiding countless scriptures in our heart is the only way we will be able to fight the good fight of faith with The Word of God as our sword, the way God designed us to fight. A broom cannot be a mop and a mop cannot be a broom. We need them both to clean effectively. We need the entire Bible saturating and penetrating our heart to be washed in the Word effectively. We can't pick and choose, or we will still feel dirty in areas.

Each scripture that God breathed is useful for us. Each scripture that God breathed is a small and intricate detail in His amazing love letter written for us called the Bible. The truth is the more we study the Word, the healthier we will become and the more obsessed we will become with getting healthier spirit, body, and soul.  It truly is the amazing obsession.

**Prayer Focus: Spend time in prayer with God asking Him for a fresh desire to read and study more of His Word.**

**Now that's 3:16 Power!**

# How Soft Is Your Heart?

## Hebrews 3:16

### *Who were they who heard and rebelled? Were they not all those Moses led out of Egypt?*

When God led the Israelites out of slavery and into the wilderness as they prepared to enter the Promised Land, they experienced countless miracles, consistent protection, and supernatural provision from the Lord. These miracles ranged from daily manna rained from Heaven to feed them, to the ability to produce water by speaking to a rock. Unfortunately, their hearts just were not moldable enough for God to work the way He wanted to in and through them. They just kept hardening their hearts. Even Moses did not follow God's plan completely by simply speaking to the rock to produce water, he called the people to watch as he tapped on the rock and spoke to it. Partial obedience to God is still disobedience. The people just kept worrying about provision, complaining about their situation and their grumbling prolonged their deliverance. God finally decided that their disobedience was not going to be rewarded and that generation was unable to enter the Promised Land.

Hard hearts prevent a lot of us from our deliverance as well. Hard hearts prevent us from seeing miracles that are still happening today for those who dare to believe. Hard hearts prevent us from healing. Hard hearts keep us in unforgiveness, bitterness and eventually bound up in strongholds of the enemy.

Our hearts must be pliable, flexible, and able to believe that whatever God says will happen, will happen. The level of our faith determines the level of our obedience and the level of our obedience determines the level of blessings we will experience. Blessings follow obedience. When our hearts are hardened by sin or unbelief God is unable to move in and through us the way He chooses to. We must soften our hearts for the garden of our hearts to produce abundant fruit that lasts.

The Israelites just could not get the fact that grumbling, complaining and negativity were the roadblocks preventing the pathway to their deliverance. We must also recognize where our stubbornness and lack of humility and obedience is blocking ours as well.

What is it? What is it that you are holding onto today that is preventing you from experiencing God's peace? How about His healing? How about hearing Him speak clearly to you? Do you need to forgive someone? Are you holding onto bitterness in an area and God clearly keeps telling you to let it go? Today, do not be hardened by sin's deceitfulness. Trust that God has your soft heart in the palm of His hands. He will protect it. He is much better at holding this world together than we are. Let it go, my friend. Soften your heart.

**Prayer focus: Spend time in prayer with God. Ask Him if your heart is hard in any area. Release it today my friend and step into your promised Land of healing.**

**Now that's 3:16 Power!**

# It Ain't All About You

## James 3:16

*For where you have envy and selfish ambition, there you find disorder and every evil practice.*

Don't you love that title, "It Ain't All About You?" It takes a true country girl to call herself an author, but still use "ain't" as if it were a preferred word choice. I am choosing to ignore all the underlining wisdom that my computer is screaming at me to try to correct my poor judgment in grammar. That kind of leads me into my object lesson in question: How teachable are you? I think you can tell by my opening, that I struggle a little with this. I have a natural inclination towards selfish ambition. My natural self (who I am when I ignore the Holy Spirit's leadership) is quite bossy and opinionated. This isn't fun to admit, but like I have said a billion times before in much of my writing and teaching, "I am a hot mess without Jesus."

I must consistently crucify my flesh that wants to compete with others and point out other's flaws and say, "It's my way or the highway." I have to daily die to my old natural self and put on my new self which is guided and directed by the Holy Spirit. If I do not choose to do this, the consequences are listed above, "there you find disorder and every evil practice." I must purposely choose to follow the leadership of the Holy Spirit. I must purposely place others' needs, desires, and ambitions ahead of mine. I must purposely crucify my jealous nature. I must purposely do these things to avoid disorder and evil in my life. Quite honestly, living humbly this way is much more peaceful, and peace is worth a lifetime of not winning arguments and disputes.

How about you? Do you struggle with envy? Are there people that you find yourself jealous of or competing against when God has placed them in your life as an acquaintance, loved one or friend? The Word says that envy and selfish ambition lead to disorder and evil practices. We see this every day in our world. Bullies don't bully because they feel good about themselves, bullies bully out of insecurity and jealousy. Bullies bully and haters hate because of selfish ambition and envy. To say we will ever actually conquer the bullying problem that we face in society is sort of ridiculous. Bullying stems from evil. Evil will always be prevalent as long as Satan is still battling against the Bride of Christ. The only way to overcome evil is to do good, and good can only come from the Holy Spirit. Bullying only is cured when the bullies meet Jesus face to face.

Envy and selfish ambition are acts of the sinful nature. Our sinful nature is selfish and self-seeking. We must crucify our old selfish nature by choosing to submit to our new nature, the Holy Spirit. We are only able to put to death envy and selfish ambition by daily renewing our minds in the Word of God and allowing our new mind to control our old nature.

Other people have much better ideas than us sometimes. Other people have different approaches to life situations than us sometimes. Other people's opinions have value. But until we can kill our old selfish ambition and vain conceit, we will miss out on receiving the benefits of learning to humbly submit to hearing and receiving these blessings.

I believe God has given all of us different pieces to this puzzle called life and if we can humble ourselves and remember that we may only have the corner pieces, we will begin to fit together in a tapestry so beautiful that our Father in Heaven will be glorified beyond measure. After all, it ain't all about us. It's about Him.

**Prayer focus: Spend time in prayer with God asking Him where you may be struggling with envy or selfish ambition.**

**Now that's 3:16 Power!**

# A Good Name

## 1 Peter 3:16

*keeping a clear conscience, so that those who speak maliciously against your good behavior in Christ may be ashamed of their slander.*

My four kids have heard me tell them countless times the proverb that I pray they will always recite and apply to their lives, "a good name is worth more than riches." (Proverbs 22:1) I would speak this over and over to them when they would come home frustrated by disagreements with friends. I would speak this to them when they would be confronted with peer pressure. I would speak this to them when they would ask why other kids were allowed to do things that they were not. I also loved to use my favorite line, "they have different parents than you." How can you argue with that?

My husband and I tried to instill it in our children to pursue safe boundaries in dating, in relationships and in life in general. We would encourage them to always date in groups so that no one could accuse you of doing something that you didn't do, which could malign your good name. I pray consistently and fervently that my husband's name, my name and my family's name will be guarded and protected from any schemes of the enemy.

The truth is, though that my name and my husband's name have been spoken against publicly in negative ways. We have had situations in ministry where people that we have loved and attempted to help or minister to have decided to allow the boundaries that we have set up to anger them enough to speak deadly venom about us on social media, to our face or through gossip. The truth is, if you are following Christ and attempting to live a holy life, you will be hurt by others and you will sometimes hurt others, intentionally and unintentionally unfortunately.

Yes, this life is tough, and people will not always be nice. But God is good, and His Word never returns void. I believe in my heart that those people who speak maliciously about others who are truthfully trying to follow God and his will for their lives eventually feel ashamed for their slander. Sometimes they apologize, but sometimes they do not.

I know that I have found myself feeling extremely convicted about judging others before I have sought to understand them fully. I have found myself asking for people's forgiveness for my unkind words plenty of times.

Peter simply encourages his readers to do good, to be prepared to give an answer for all of those who wonder where your hope comes from and to keep a clear conscience. He lets us know that our good name will convict them of their slander. Our good name will be our ally and defense. We don't have to fight back. We simply must overcome evil with good and seek peace and pursue it.

It never feels good when people say negative things about us. It never feels good when people throw stones. Jesus knew just how we feel. They hurled insults at Him and mocked Him and spit on His holy name. As Christ followers, we will face persecution. But friend, they will eventually feel ashamed to slander those that bear the Name of Christ and attempt to live like Christ. Hold fast and hold onto your good reputation. It is worth more than riches.

**Prayer focus: Spend time in prayer with God asking Him what you can do to protect your good name and who you may need to apologize to for things you have said or done to malign others good name.**

**Now that's 3:16 power!**

# What You Don't Know Could Kill You

## 2 Peter 3:16

*He writes the same way in all his letters, speaking in them of these matters. His letters contain some things that are hard to understand, which ignorant and unstable people distort, as they do the other Scriptures, to their own destruction.*

What we don't know could kill us. Ignorance is not bliss. Ignorance is dangerous. Peter is discussing the return of Christ in the last chapter of 2 Peter. He is warning God's people to make every effort to be found blameless and spotless as the day of the Lord will come like a thief in the night. He was talking about Paul's letters and how Paul warns us of this often in his letters, but instead of seeking to know the truth, many distorted the truth because they were too ignorant to seek to understand the truth. Their ignorance would be to their demise.

Ignorance always robs us; it never protects us. The Word says in Proverbs 4:7: "The beginning of wisdom is this: Get wisdom. Though it cost all you have, get understanding." Wisdom protects us from the truth being distorted. Distorted truth is, simply put, lies. The enemy loves when we begin to believe lies because believing lies keeps us from God's best for us.

Throughout history, ignorant and unstable people who have failed to seek wisdom and truth for themselves have found themselves trapped in Satan's web of deceit which leads to an eventual road paved straight to his plan: to kill, steal and destroy us. The sad thing is, one generation's inability to seek wisdom and truth for themselves sometimes leads to multiple generational ignorance that continues until someone's spiritual eyes are eventually opened by seeking wisdom.

Prejudices, hatred, poor doctrines and "man-made traditions" are often passed down from one generation to the next because of ignorance and a failure to seek wisdom. We do things and believe things, not even knowing why. We simply have "always done it this way." Not seeking an understanding of why we do what we do and why we believe what we believe is continuing a pattern of ignorance like the one that Peter is talking about, that will cause destruction.

Salvation and correct doctrine and biblical truths on every subject are all available to us in God's Word. We simply must seek to find the truth ourselves. We cannot simply rely on the words and wisdom passed down from Granny or Sister so and so. We must make sure that we go to God's Word and accept whatever lines up with biblical truth and deny whatever does not stand up to truth.

The lies of the enemy are not always packaged in a box straight from our enemy's mouth. Sometimes the lies that we believe were fed to us by those we love and respect the most. We must become diligent students of the Word to be able to correctly decipher what are lies and what is truth.

Yes, Granny usually has a ton of wisdom to offer us. Yes, Granny's prayers have probably rescued us many times from our own pits that we would have found ourselves in, in life. But make sure Granny knows her Word, because ignorance is not bliss and wisdom is supreme. Though is cost you all you have, get understanding.

**Prayer focus: Spend time in prayer with God asking Him to show you areas that you may be believing things that do not line up with the Word of God.**

**Now that's 3:16 Power!**

## Laying Down Our Lives

### 1 John 3:16

*This is how we know what love is: Jesus Christ laid down his life for us. And we ought to lay down our lives for our brothers and sisters.*

How do we lay down our lives for others? Is the Apostle John speaking figuratively or are we literally going to have to take a bullet for those we love? My answer is, maybe both. Thank God for the men and women who sacrifice their lives for the freedom that we take for granted so often as Americans. Thank God for the missionaries in closed countries who risk imprisonment, slavery, and death to fulfill The Great Commission to take God's love to the world. Yes, thank God for heroes and martyrs of the past and of today, who literally lay down their lives for the gospel.

I also believe that John is also talking about you and me laying down our material possessions, our agendas, our wills, and our opinions so that we can genuinely love others as Christ loves us. I believe John is speaking to you and me who may struggle sometimes sharing that new lawnmower or boat with our neighbors that we have been saving for and finally purchased. I think John is saying, *lay down the fear that they may break it. Lay down the 80 rules you are going to hand them before you "graciously" let them borrow it.*

1 John 3:16 is talking about loving like Jesus loved. Jesus loved sacrificially. Jesus loved unconditionally. Jesus loved with no hidden agenda. He simply loved. He was okay being interrupted. How do we do with that? Do we love pop-ins when we are trying to get our to-do list finished? I know I struggle with my plans being changed at the last minute. Jesus looked at these changes as opportunities to minister, and we need to as well.

As Jesus was on His way to minister to a synagogue leader's daughter who was dying, He was interrupted in a busy crowd by the woman with the issue of blood. She reached out and touched His garment and her bleeding disorder that she had suffered with for twelve years was immediately cured. Jesus did not rebuke the woman for her interruption. He said, "Daughter, your faith has healed you." Jesus encouraged her perseverance. This "interruption" was no interruption at all. It was a holy encounter.

We must learn to be this way in loving our brothers and sisters. Their needs will not always fit into our perfect little helping schedule. Their need to talk to you, cry with you, or even require a word of encouragement from you may not be able to wait until Thursday between 12:00 and 1:00 o'clock when you have blocked out "ministry time". Loving our brothers and sisters in Christ the way that Jesus loved, requires us to drop our own agendas sometimes.

Laying down our lives for our brothers and sisters and laying down our lives for the cause of Christ is how we know what real love is. Real love involves sacrifice. Real love involves giving. Sometimes we give of our things. Sometimes we give of our wisdom. Sometimes we give of our time. Laying down our lives means letting God truly rule and reign in our lives.

When we can truly learn to surrender our entire lives to loving God and loving people, we will then begin to experience joy beyond our wildest dreams. A life lived well for God and others is a life of purpose. You see, we find a life, an amazing life, when we finally learn to lay ours down.

**Prayer focus: Spend time in prayer with God asking Him who you can love and help today.**

**Now that's 3:16 Power!**

# Hot Coffee, Please

## Revelation 3:16

*So, because you are lukewarm-neither hot nor cold-I am about to spit you out of my mouth.*

I bet God likes coffee. I know I won't know this until I get to Heaven, but He seems like a coffee drinker to me. Coffee drinkers know how they like their coffee. True coffee drinkers don't get up to the speaker in the drive-thru and wonder what they are going to order. True coffee drinkers know how they like their coffee, the temperature they want their coffee and what time of day is the best for them to drink their coffee. True coffee drinkers are serious about one thing. It better be hot or cold. Lukewarm coffee might as well be spit out.

I love God's passion. I love His zeal. I love His desire that we live our lives full of passion and zeal ourselves. When the Lord speaks to the church at Laodicea in Revelation, He is speaking to us as well. He says, "I know your deeds, that you are neither cold nor hot." How true this is of us in so many areas of our walk with Christ.

We are hot on Sundays. We have our arms lifted high in praise and worship. We bombard the altar wanting to follow God wholeheartedly. We want to please Him, honor Him, follow Him into the battle to save the lost. Then Wednesday comes at work and we spend our afternoon stealing company time surfing the internet instead of working.

Then we are hot again on Wednesday night at Bible study. We want to see our neighbors reached with the gospel. We want to help widows and orphans. We want to be Jesus to a lost world. Then Friday night comes around and we head out drinking with the girls for "ladies' night." After all, "Jesus turned water into wine, so, what's the big deal, right?"

The big deal is, we are lukewarm. We lack the spiritual fervor needed to say no to the things God wants us to say no to and yes to the things that He wants us to scream yes to. God is looking for some on-fire Christians who will say, "As for me and my house, we will serve the Lord." God is looking for some saints who will choose to take the narrow road instead of selling out and taking the wide road that many are on that leads to destruction.

The Lord wants us hot or cold, not lukewarm. He wants us to care about our testimony and our witness the same way we care about how many squirts of French vanilla get put in our latte. God wants us caring so much about reaching the lost world with the gospel that we will stop being lukewarm and heat up a little. God wants us to reignite the fire on the altar of our heart and stop letting it go out every other day.

How do we do this? We live and breathe and move and have our being in Him. We dig into His Word and devour it like food. We crucify our flesh daily and we choose to fix our eyes on Jesus and work at looking more and more like Him every day. We live hot or cold and not lukewarm by doing what we did at first, falling in love with Jesus and making a decision that He is not only Savior of our lives, He is also Lord, and Lord means boss.

Let's fan the flame that the Holy Spirit is aching to set ablaze in our hearts. Let's learn to live for Jesus the way we love our coffee, hot or cold, never lukewarm.

**Prayer focus: Spend time in prayer with God asking Him to show you where you are living a little lukewarm. Then, repent.**

**Now that's 3:16 Power!**

Dear Reader,

I am humbled and thankful that you took time to read and study one of my books. As always, I pray that God's Word came alive to you in such a supernatural way that you will never be the same.

Every day that we are here on earth it is our privilege to read and study and allow God's Word to change us and make us more like Jesus. It is an honor to be a Christ follower and I pray that this devotional drew you closer than ever to our Savior Jesus.

Truly, the only thing that matters to me in this world is that I have loved God and loved people correctly. I pray that you felt that love as you read and studied with me throughout this powerful journey.

Now that's 3:16 Power!

God bless you,

Mo Mydlo

Made in USA - Kendallville, IN
34663_9798666489420
03.17.2022 1405